VIETNAMESE FOOD
any day

VIETNAMESE FOOD
any day

Simple recipes for true, fresh flavors

ANDREA NGUYEN

Photographs by Aubrie Pick

TEN SPEED PRESS
California | New York

CONTENTS

SEEDS OF MY SUPERMARKET OBSESSION

Around the corner from my childhood home in Saigon was an open-air market. It stretched along a narrow road for a full block, emptying out onto a busy thoroughfare. Our lanky cook, whom we respectfully addressed as Older Sister Thien, regularly took me there. I was her food-shopping pal. The market was huge and noisy, with vendors hawking dry goods, vibrant produce, freshly butchered meats, and live seafood. Some vendors sat high on platforms while others were close to the ground. They'd often beckon to me in order to pat a chubby child, a rarity in early 1970s Vietnam. They'd check in and joke with Older Sister Thien while I stood nearby feeling awkward with nothing to do. To busy myself, I studied the beautifully arranged tropical fruits and vegetables, which looked like jewels meant to attract and charm customers. Fish splashing around in tubs were always extra-exciting. People carefully selecting ingredients and negotiating their transactions with the vendors intrigued me. Those market visits seeded my interests in food, cooking, and grocery shopping.

Fast forward to May 1975 and the first time my family checked out an American supermarket. We were new refugee arrivals who'd just fled Vietnam's political upheaval. My parents were relieved, yet wary about how they'd build new lives. I gleefully marched down the meat aisle and did something that I'd always wanted to do back at the market by our house—touch and poke every package within my short arm's reach. Aghast and embarrassed, my mom scowled and restrained me with a firm grip. I stopped. Disciplining me distracted her from perusing the supermarket's offerings and trying to figure out how she could make the most from ingredients at hand. It was months before we got a car to make the three-hour-roundtrip drive to Los Angeles's Chinatown, where we'd load up on familiar Asian staples.

The Albertsons supermarket was a walkable distance from the apartment we rented and became our neighborhood store. Shopping there meant certain compromises on ingredients. Fish sauce wasn't carried at mainstream American markets in the '70s, and we initially relied upon La Choy soy sauce. From bags of Texas long-grain rice, cheap chicken backs, onion, ginger, and celery, we simmered fragrant stock, saved the rendered fat, and picked off the meat in order to fashion pots of glorious chicken and celery rice (see page 189). Bittersweet caramel sauce (see page 32), a Viet staple for simmering ingredients such as chunks of fatty pork to a super-savory finish, was easy to make with granulated sugar. We were happy to find plenty of lettuce, cilantro, and mint to eat with grilled and fried morsels.

Working the phone lines and sharing tips with other refugees, my mom co-opted non-Viet ingredients for Viet dishes. For example, Mochiko sweet rice flour produced by Koda Farms, a Japanese American family in Central California, yielded outrageously good Vietnamese sticky rice cakes and soft, chewy filled dumplings. For decades, she substituted Swans Down cake flour for rice flour to make *bánh cuốn* steamed rice rolls. Like many good cooks, my mom adapted her cooking for her current situation. In the process, she and other Vietnamese immigrants helped evolve and advance their food traditions. Incorporating American work-arounds while not compromising Vietnamese integrity created foodways that helped to define the Vietnamese American experience.

Our eating life improved once we were able to stock up on fish sauce, rice noodles, and rice paper at Chinese markets, and eventually at Little Saigon grocers in Westminster and Garden Grove, towns located about thirty-five miles away. However, the convenience of having nearby Viet ingredients, delis, and restaurants didn't motivate us to move to a Vietnamese American enclave, so we had to create our favorite foods at home. From the get-go, my parents wanted our family to assimilate into American society and they were clear in their approach—master English for everyday life; but at home, speak and eat mostly Vietnamese. Spaghetti dinners included a side of rice.

Keeping our feet in two worlds was an adventure, not a challenge. We were thrifty but well fed. My mom read the weekly supermarket circular ads like they were the Bible. Then, she made a list and sent my dad and me to various markets to score grocery deals all over town. In at least one store, we'd inevitably check the produce department for discounted overripe bananas to make a cake like the one on page 215. Ditto for the bargain shelves of closeouts or nearly expired foods. We also tried unfamiliar, "exotic" foods like Hostess fruit pies and strawberry-flavored Nesquik to mix with milk, and other packaged prepared offerings. Still, we also regularly stopped at Vermeulen's farm stand for fruit and produce. And for fun and freshness, my dad grew lemongrass, mint, and several other herbs. That's how I learned to honor our culture yet stay open-minded, cook on a budget, and appreciate nature's bounty. Those values have served me well.

/

When I wrote my first cookbook, *Into the Vietnamese Kitchen*, interest in the food of Vietnam was nascent and mainly occupied foodies and culinary geeks like me. Many of the ingredients called for were available at supermarkets, but to present the richness of Vietnamese cuisine I had to ask cooks to shop at Asian markets for a specific quality of fish sauce and noodles. I was trying to stay as true as possible to the flavors and textures of traditional dishes, all the while reflecting my experiences as a Vietnamese American. A lot has changed since that book released in 2006. An uptick in media coverage of Vietnamese food in print, television, and online made it trendy. Tourism and business in Vietnam increased—former president Barack Obama met up with Anthony Bourdain in Hanoi to sample *bún chả* (grilled pork with rice noodles and herbs, see page 201). Sriracha, a Thai hot sauce that had become a mainstay at Viet restaurants, has practically become an American staple. Even tofu has gained wider acceptance. My cookbooks on banh mi and pho, released, respectively, in 2014 and 2017, spotlighted Vietnam's signature dishes in traditional and modern incarnations. (Mexican bolillo rolls are fabulous for Viet sandwiches! Pressure cookers make pho doable for weeknight eating!) Writing those books for a broader audience meant spending more time where most Americans shop for food—the supermarket. And being a busy writer, I also learned how to fit good, interesting food into hectic lifestyles.

In my hometown of Santa Cruz, California, as well as cities I've visited, I noticed a steady change in the Asian food sections of local supermarkets; there was a much greater variety, which went beyond the usual suspects of Chinese and Japanese soy products. More important, I could purchase brands that I used to find only at Asian markets, such as Chaokoh coconut milk; Sun brand's Madras-style curry powder, a family favorite, could be found in the regular spice aisle; and quality white and quick-cooking brown jasmine rice were in the Asian aisle *and* regular rice section.

/

The diversification of American supermarkets has been tremendous. According to the Food Marketing Institute (a trade group), in 1975, super-markets carried about 9,000 products. Today, the average supermarket has roughly 40,000 items. Too many choices can confound (which is why cell phones are common grocery-shopping lifelines), but I see them as an oppor-tunity to help cooks shop wisely and mine the resources at their fingertips to make good Vietnamese food. For example, trends in gluten-free and whole foods nudged pasta companies to develop white and brown rice capellini and spaghetti—terrific subs for traditional Vietnamese *bún* (round rice noodles). I use rice spaghetti for Spicy Hue Noodle Soup (*bún bò Huế*, page 89), and the capellini is great for rice paper rolls (see page 119), lettuce wraps (see page 139), and rice noodle salad bowls (see page 197). Pomegranate molasses (see page 34) and juice are my tart-sweet stand-in for tamarind, which has yet to be widely distributed. Fresh turmeric, coconut water, and coconut oil may be new health-boosting ingredients to some people, but to me, they're game changers for creating vibrant flavors that beautifully capture what I've enjoyed in Vietnam.

Realizing that a wider array of Viet dishes can be part of the American table, I decided to write *Vietnamese Food Any Day* based on ingredients found at most mainstream market chains such as Kroger, Whole Foods, Albertsons, Trader Joe's, Publix, and Giant Eagle. I've also canvassed Costco and Walmart. And whenever possible, I've scoped out well-stocked inde-pendent markets too. Given the reasonable inventory overlap between mainstream and ethnic grocers, there's no Asian-market shopping required for this book. That said, this book's approach to showcasing Vietnamese cuisine isn't hodgepodge. It's based on a Vietnamese term, *khéo*, that means "smart" and "adroit," but when applied to cooking, it conveys food that's been thoughtfully and skillfully prepared with intention and a grounding in the fundamentals.

In the spirit of *khéo* cooking, the recipes herein are streamlined but not dumbed down. They capture the essence of Vietnamese foodways, while demystifying and decoding the cuisine for home cooks. Simple recipes that I've gathered from Vietnam, such as the Grilled Slashed Chicken on page 98, underscore the cuisine's possibilities. On the other hand, reimagined classics prepared with nontraditional ingredients, such as the Smoked Turkey Pho on page 84, will inspire you to improvise. Developed to be fun and/or low-stress, the recipes are prepared with regular pots and pans (no wok or Chinese steamer is required), a pressure cooker, and a microwave oven. There's no deep-frying, because as much as many of us love eating fried food, few of us want to make it and clean up afterward.

We're cooking and eating in very exciting times. The tumultuous history of Vietnam, informed by its regional differences, varied topography, and extensive interactions with foreign peoples through colonial occupation, war, and diaspora, laid the foundation for a lot of make-do cooking. Viet cooks are curious and inventive by nature. They're always creating new dishes, incorporating new ingredients, or reconsidering old-fashioned, labor-intensive techniques. That dynamic keeps the cuisine and culture evolving. This cookbook will help you plug into that mindset to make Vietnamese food. Through preparing recipes in *Vietnamese Food Any Day*, you'll come to understand how Vietnamese flavors may be built, how to put together a Vietnamese meal, and how to incorporate Vietnamese cooking into your repertoire. Viet food doesn't have to be an exotic, special weekend project. It's deliciously doable whenever you want.

VIETNAMESE VS. *VIỆT*—WHAT'S THE DIFFERENCE?

In this book and my everyday speech, I employ *Vietnamese* and *Viet* interchangeably to describe anything Vietnamese. However, *Việt* has a little edge because to Viet people it has historically signaled national pride and self-determination. Whenever Vietnam was able to free itself from the colonial domination of the Chinese or French, it called its territory Viet *something* (Nam Viet, Viet Nam) to underscore its resistance and resilience. Get into the Viet spirit by adding the term to your vocabulary.

The organization of this book explained

Cookbooks are like technical manuals; the front of the book presents the ground rules, and this cookbook is no exception. There's guidance for sourcing and selecting commonly used staples, as well as recipes and blueprints for essentials in the Vietnamese kitchen. That content will help you master Viet cuisine and perhaps up your cooking game too. Check out the section on Strategic Shopping for Ingredients (page 11) and the Basic Recipes and Know-How chapter, and then dig into the rest of the book.

As you cook through the recipes, remember to:

- Peruse the headnotes (recipe introductions) for cultural and technical tidbits.

- Pick recipes that match your interests and availability. In general, the shorter ones require less effort. Recipe time estimates include active and passive cooking times to help you determine your overall commitment. Use make-ahead tips to manage long recipes (break them into smaller tasks and do some in advance!). We all cook at difference paces, and your first try at making something new may take a little longer.

- Scan a recipe's instructions and Notes section for extra insights. You may find pointers on equipment, ingredients, and suitable substitutes. Reheating information and lifespan clues on how long a finished dish keeps are cues for planning leftover lunches, parties, and potlucks. Recipe variations are often tucked into the Notes.

Menu planning

To assemble recipes from this book into a traditional Viet meal, pick a soup (the mustard greens one on page 68 is a terrific quickie) and a main dish (featuring meat, seafood, eggs, or tofu), then add a salad or vegetable side and serve with rice; omit the soup if you're short on time. Or, pluck one or two recipes to accompany non-Vietnamese dishes, for example, pair Honey-Glazed Pork Riblets (page 125) and Green Mango, Cabbage, and Jicama Salad (page 163) with a potato salad for a summertime meal. A handful of recipes are one-dish wonders, such as Grilled Trout Rice Paper Rolls (page 119) and a Rice Noodle Salad Bowl (page 197), that may play the starring role of a fun brunch, lunch, or dinner. The savory snacks can plug into a nosh session or cocktail party. And the sweets are great for an afternoon tea break or post-dinner treat.

This collection of recipes is built for versatility and creativity. When cooking and eating in our American home, my family often enjoys cross-cultural menus. You should too.

How to use recipes like a pro

Using a recipe well does not require following it slavishly but rather thoughtfully interpreting it for your situation. A recipe is like a roadmap filled with signposts to guide you on a culinary journey. You may make a wrong turn or elect to take a detour, but you'll arrive at your destination and create your own personal path along the way—if you keep a few things in mind.

To turn my recipes into yours:

- Organize your work for the greatest efficiency. The list of ingredients in any recipe is presented in the order in which the ingredients are used, which isn't necessarily the most logical order of prep. For example, identify and do advance prep work, such as making stocks or sauces, boiling noodles, and washing lettuce and herbs. If you use one cutting board for all your chopping, prep the vegetables before the raw proteins to minimize mess and cross-contamination. Ingredients that will be thrown into the pan together may be kept in the same bowl. Why dirty up extra dishes?

- Measure your ingredients with care. Use volume and liquid measuring cups as needed and use a scale (best when baking) because it never lies.

- Know your burners. All the recipes in this book were developed and tested by me, and then cross-tested by an intrepid team of volunteers. We cook on home kitchen stoves. If the range was gas, the burners were between 9,000 and 12,000 BTUs. If you're cooking on burners with even more power, your cooking time may be faster than the time suggested in the recipe. Use the visual and tactile cues to guide your progress, and lower the heat as needed.

- Have everything ready when fast-cooking (think stir-frying) is involved. Line up the prepped ingredients by the stove, and keep needed equipment at hand so you can flow through the motions.

- The first time through, follow the recipe to understand the parameters and benchmarks. When you've adjusted it to your liking, jot down your changes.

Essential equipment

To make food from this book, you don't have to outfit your kitchen with unusual gadgets. You'll employ tools and appliances such as a digital scale, food processor (small and regular size), blender, pressure cooker, and microwave oven. Along with the saucepans and skillets in the following chart, a cast-iron stove-top grill pan will also be useful, and a few recipes have you grilling outdoors. In other words, you'll be using ordinary kitchen equipment for extraordinary food.

STANDARD COOKING VESSEL SIZES

	SAUCEPAN	SKILLET
SMALL	1- to 1½-quart capacity	8-inch wide
MEDIUM	2- to 3-quart capacity	10-inch wide
LARGE	4-quart capacity	12-inch wide

Note: A "large pot" should hold five quarts or more, enough to boil a bunch of noodles or cook a braise or stew. When critical, recipes will indicate capacity.

MULTICOOKERS VS. PRESSURE COOKERS

Multicookers are electric programmable pressure cookers. Designed for stove-top cooking, regular pressure cookers have smaller footprints and are easy to operate. I own both kinds. The beauty of multicookers is that you can set them to work and they'll maintain pressure and cook according to your specified time; you don't have to monitor them. The hardest thing to learn on multicookers is which buttons to push. As an assist, I include guidance for two popular models, the Fagor Lux and the Instant Pot, which are my personal favorites.

STRATEGIC SHOPPING FOR INGREDIENTS

Now more than ever, American supermarkets are offering a stupendous range of ingredients for global flavors. That's why *none* of the recipes in this book requires a trip to an Asian market.

Where to start searching for ingredients? Mine your local grocers and retailers to see what's available. Each store's inventory reflects its customer base and location (Kroger markets are not all the same, for example). Explore regular supermarkets, Whole Foods, Trader Joe's, Costco, farmers' markets, savvy neighborhood markets, health food stores, ethnic markets, and even Cost Plus World Market. When you can't find something, ask for it. Grocery-store staff are knowledgeable and accommodating; they'll point you to the best cuts of meat, order things for you, and perhaps suggest another store that stocks what you need. Shop like my mother, a sharp woman in her eighties, and demand service. If you can't get what you want, it's time to try another market or look online.

This ingredients guide is organized like the aisles of most conventional markets. Inventories are always changing, so I occasionally mention seemingly esoteric but very good brands found at select mainstream grocers; maybe they'll be widely available someday. Look to brand suggestions, tasting notes, and photos like the one opposite to help you shop.

Asian ingredients

Head to the Asian foods aisle and peruse the shelves, from high to low. Some things are also stocked in other parts of the grocery store. Products sold under a store's own label are often the same as name-brand versions. Compare ingredients lists and nutrition labels. Keep an open mind. Think of this as a scavenger hunt!

Condiments

CHILE GARLIC SAUCE

Of all the chile garlic sauces commercially made, the one with a good balance of moderate heat and tang is produced by Huy Fong and labeled *tương ớt tỏi Việt-Nam* (Vietnamese chile garlic sauce). It's widely distributed but you can also make your own version with the recipe on page 31. When you don't have the sauce handy, substitute sambal oelek, an earthy hot sauce crafted for Indonesian and Malay dishes, or use sriracha.

> BRAND / Huy Fong (the "rooster brand")

FISH SAUCE

Most savory Viet dishes rely upon this umami-laden seasoning for their signature flavors. Fish sauce smells strong (the good stuff is heady, like dried porcini), but it's commonly combined with other ingredients. Embrace *nước mắm*. Check the ingredients list if you're gluten-sensitive. Refrigerate fish sauce if you don't use it often; should it darken and intensify in flavor, use a little less than the amount suggested in a recipe.

> BRANDS / Red Boat (artisanal), Three Crabs (Việt Hương; a perennial favorite, a little saltier than others), Megachef (salty-sweet, labeled "anchovy sauce"), Dynasty and Thai Taste (both are earthy, savory), Thai Kitchen (flat tasting, but perfectly usable for this book)

HOISIN SAUCE

Made from fermented soybeans, sweet-salty-spicy hoisin is often used in marinades and dipping sauces.

> BRAND / Lee Kum Kee (a popular, reliable brand)

MAGGI SEASONING SAUCE OR BRAGG LIQUID AMINOS

Introduced by French colonials, Maggi Seasoning sauce lends a unique meaty flavor to food and is key for great banh mi. Bragg Liquid Aminos, a health food favorite, is often shelved with Asian ingredients. Supermarkets with a strong Asian or Latino clientele tend to carry Maggi.

OYSTER SAUCE

Thick and salty-sweet oyster sauce is employed in stir-fries and other dishes. To underscore the condiment's piscine notes, combine it with a little fish sauce.

BRANDS / Lee Kum Kee (their Panda brand is good, but the premium label, which depicts a woman and boy in a boat, is better), Kikkoman (very good with no MSG), Dynasty (less salty than others, so use about 25 percent more)

RICE VINEGAR

Choose an unseasoned rice vinegar from Japan for vibrant, clean flavor. In addition to a store's Asian foods section, check the regular vinegar selection, near the cooking oils.

BRANDS / Marukan (excellent bright flavor), Mizkan and Kikkoman (good, slightly milder flavor)

SESAME OIL

Look for toasted (dark) sesame oil. Those from Japan have a fabulous, deep flavor.

BRANDS / Dynasty, Kadoya, Spectrum (in the regular oil section)

SOY SAUCE

This Chinese condiment lends savory goodness to many Viet dishes. Use full-sodium soy sauce for recipes in this book.

BRANDS / Kikkoman (regular or gluten-free), Pearl River Bridge (light or superior light), Lee Kum Kee

SRIRACHA

Originally made in Thailand, this hot sauce is now associated with pho and other Vietnamese dishes. Its tangy, garlicky heat varies among brands. American-made versions, such as Huy Fong's, are more assertive than ones made in Thailand and Vietnam.

BRANDS / Huy Fong, Fusia (well balanced, an Aldi brand), Fix (bold, garlicky flavor)

Dried noodles and rice

CHINESE WHEAT NOODLES

As Vietnam's northern neighbor, China heavily influences Viet culture and cuisine. That's why these wheat-based noodles (*mì* in Vietnamese; *mein* in Chinese) are used for many Chinese-style noodle soups, stir-fries, and pan-fried and deep-fried dishes. The noodles cook up tender-chewy (not al dente, like Italian pasta) and are made with or without egg. When unavailable, ramen is a great substitute.

> BRANDS / Golden Dragon, Wel-Pac

FLAT RICE NOODLES (PAD THAI NOODLES)

Called *bánh phở* in Vietnamese, these flat noodles are practically synonymous with pho, Vietnam's national dish. In this book, you'll use them for the Smoked Turkey Pho on page 84. Look for noodles that are as wide as linguine or fettuccine. (In a pinch, use flat rice noodles for round rice noodles.)

> BRANDS / Three Ladies and Sun Voi (sold at Asian markets and, occasionally, mainstream grocers), Annie Chun, Taste of Thai

GLASS NOODLES (SAIFUN AND BEAN THREAD NOODLES)

These gluten-free noodles are made from mung bean starch. Called *miến* in Vietnamese, they're commonly sold in bundles about the size of a Twinkie: A 1.5-ounce bundle measures about 2 inches wide, 4½ inches long, and 1¼ inches thick. Although they look inedible when you take them out of the package, they're magical. During the cooking process, the noodles become supple, turning clear and plumping up as they absorb the surrounding liquid and flavors. To prep, soften in hot water and then use scissors or a knife to cut them up. These noodles go by many names in English; *saifun* is the Chinese name often seen on packages.

> BRANDS / Dynasty, Golden Star, Ka-me, and Lungkow (with a twin dragon logo, sold at Asian markets and, occasionally, mainstream grocers)

RICE, JASMINE

White long-grain rice is what most Vietnamese people prepare for everyday meals. For terrific flavor and aroma, select jasmine rice, either white or brown. Jasmine rice grown in Thailand is consistently excellent; brown Thai jasmine often cooks faster than its American counterpart. Shop for jasmine rice in the regular rice section and Asian section.

BRANDS / Three Ladies (my usual, available at Cost Plus World Market and Asian markets), Dynasty, Golden Star, Lotus Foods, Trader Joe's, 365 Everyday Value (Whole Foods brand)

RICE PAPER

American supermarkets tend to carry only one brand of rice paper (*bánh tráng*), so use the one that's sold where you shop. If you don't like it, try another market. In general, brands that list rice first have better flavor. They usually include tapioca starch for a supple texture and a product that softens relatively quickly. Medium (8-inch) rice papers are the standard; if you buy smaller ones, use less filling for each roll and make more!

BRANDS / Three Ladies (my favorite, sold at Cost Plus World Market and Asian markets)

ROUND RICE NOODLES (MAIFUN)

Made mostly of rice and water plus some starch, these round rice noodles are the basis for rice noodle bowls and other favorite dishes. In Vietnamese, they are called *bún,* but packages of the dried wiry noodles may say rice sticks, rice noodles, rice vermicelli, or *maifun* (a Chinese name). They come in various sizes: fine (vermicelli), thin (capellini), medium (thin spaghetti), and thick (spaghetti). The sizing isn't part of the labeling, so eyeball the size.

With exception to the Spicy Hue Noodle Soup on page 89, which requires thick noodles, you'll be using *thin* ones; fine rice noodles are too delicate for recipes in this book but will work in a pinch. When the ideal thin ones aren't available in the Asian foods aisle, search the regular or gluten-free pasta section for capellini or thin spaghetti made from *all rice* (when other grains are blended in, the flavor isn't good for Viet dishes). During cooking, Asian noodles nearly triple in weight, whereas Western pastas double in weight; so if you're substituting Western noodles, use more of them.

BRANDS / Dynasty and Ka-me (in the Asian section); Tinkyáda, Jovial, and Trader Joe's (shelved with pasta or gluten-free products); Three Ladies and Sailing Boat (sold at Asian markets and, occasionally, mainstream grocers)

YOUR INTERNATIONAL VIETNAMESE PANTRY

Viet cooking overlaps and blends many cuisines, which means that ingredients may come from many countries. Stay culturally open-minded at the supermarket to select the best. If there's something from Vietnam, try it. In general, you'll be looking for Asian, North American, and European products. Use the multilingual labels as a language learning opportunity.

This photo captures some of the ingredients you'll be soon using. They're the kind of foodstuffs employed for recipes in this book, and they come from Canada, China, Italy, Japan, Taiwan, Thailand, Vietnam, and the United States. The condiments and spices pictured on page 10 are similarly diverse and suitable for making delicious Vietnamese food!

Produce section or farmers' market

CHILES

Maintain a small supply of Thai, jalapeño, Fresno, or serrano chiles in the fridge, where they'll stay fresh for up to 1 week. To keep for up to 1 year, give the chiles a quick pat down with a damp paper towel, let them dry, transfer to an airtight container or zipper-top plastic bag, and store in the freezer. See page 31 for tips on hot chiles. Unless directed otherwise in a recipe, retain the chile seeds to enliven dishes.

FRESH HERBS (CILANTRO, MINT, BASIL, AND MORE)

Viet food would not be as vibrant without zippy fresh herbs—cilantro is most commonly used; mint is added for refreshing notes. That's all you really need. Sprigs of cilantro and mint may be washed, spun dry, and refrigerated in separate zipper-top plastic bags with a paper towel in each one for up to 1 week. You may also trim off ½ inch from the stem end, stand the herbs in about 1½ inches of water, loosely cover with a thin plastic bag, and keep in the fridge. Change the water every few days to keep them perky. Regardless of what type you have, basil is best washed right before using. If the sprigs are droopy, trim ½ inch off the stems, and float the sprigs in a bowl of cool water for about 10 minutes to rehydrate before spinning. If available, try different herbs, such as Vietnamese coriander (*rau răm*), which has a spicy cilantro finish, or basil varieties such as Thai, lemon, or opal that offer citrus, spicy cinnamon, and anise notes, respectively.

GARLIC

To speed up prep, peel one or two heads of garlic and refrigerate the cloves in an airtight container for up to 1 week. Or, buy pre-peeled garlic. Garlic cloves come in different sizes but in general, one medium clove yields 1 teaspoon of chopped or minced, ¾ teaspoon of minced and mashed, and ½ teaspoon pressed. A large garlic clove yields 50 percent more and a small one yields 50 percent less. Unless specified, recipes call for average, medium garlic cloves.

GINGER

Select heavy hands of robust ginger with smooth skin and as few little side knobs as possible (they're extra work to peel). Ginger with good flavor often has bright-yellow flesh; break off a piece to check. Ginger varies in thickness and density; 1 ounce of chubby ginger is about 1 inch long. If desired, weigh ginger to ensure you have enough zing. Refrigerate unpeeled ginger in a plastic bag in the produce drawer, where it will keep for up to 4 weeks.

GREEN ONION
Measuring from the white root base, a small green onion is a good ¼ inch in diameter, a medium one is about ⅜ inch, and a large one is ½ inch or bigger. See page 121 for prep tips.

LEMONGRASS
Buy firm, rigid stalks and check the cut bottoms for freshness. Measured at its thickest point, a medium stalk is about ½ inch wide, and a hefty one is about ¾ inch wide. After trimming, one medium lemongrass stalk yields 2 tablespoons chopped or 1½ tablespoons grated lemongrass. Keep lemongrass refrigerated in a plastic bag for up to 1 week, or trim and freeze for up to 3 months. Fresh is best, but you can get by with lemongrass paste, sold in tubes. See page 156 for a detailed lemongrass lowdown.

LETTUCE
Soft-leaf lettuce, and occasionally crisp ones, are used for lettuce wraps, rice paper rolls, and even noodle soup. To minimize waste, wash lettuce and spin it dry soon after bringing it home or harvesting from the garden. Put the cleaned leaves in zipper-top plastic bags or recycled plastic containers designed for salad greens. Add a paper towel to absorb moisture and then refrigerate. Washed lettuce leaves will keep for up to 1 week.

SHALLOT
Shallots have a more complex flavor than regular onions. And they vary in size; for example, small ones are about the size of a key lime while a large one can be roughly equivalent to a medium-small lemon. Use the recipe measurements to check quantities, and choose firm, solid shallots.

YELLOW ONION
A small (4- to 5-ounce) yellow onion is the size of racquetball; a medium (6- to 8-ounce) one is tennis or baseball size; and a large (10- to 11-ounce) onion approaches the size of a softball.

Spice section or bulk spice section

CHINESE FIVE-SPICE POWDER
When warm, earthy notes are needed, Viet cooks deploy Chinese five-spice powder. It should smell savory-sweet with a pungent note.

BRAND / Spicely

CURRY POWDER, MADRAS-STYLE
Experiment with different blends of curry powder to find your ideal. My favorite is Sun, which lists sweet-citrusy coriander as the first ingredient. It also contains salt. If yours does not, add a little salt to recipes.

BRAND / Sun

PEPPER, BLACK AND WHITE
Store-bought ground pepper is meh. I recommend grinding peppercorns yourself for the best flavor. For efficient cooking, pre-grind your pepper—described as *recently ground* pepper in my recipes—as part of your prep work. Use a basic (inexpensive) electric coffee grinder dedicated to spices, grind whole peppercorns in small batches (start with 2 tablespoons), and see how long it lasts. Clean the grinder by grinding and discarding 2 teaspoons of raw rice. Employ a pepper mill for garnishing and table use. Indian Tellicherry peppercorns are top-notch, but Vietnam exports pepper too. If you love pepper, peruse spice shops as well as favorite markets.

BRANDS / Costco, Spicely, 365 Everyday Value (Whole Foods brand)

SALT
Fine sea salt has a clean flavor, and its texture matches what most Viet cooks use. The brands I use have 550 to 590 mg of sodium per ¼ teaspoon. If yours has less, then use a little more salt. If you use kosher salt, double the quantity in the recipe.

BRANDS / Hain, La Baleine, 365 Everyday Value (Whole Foods brand)

SETTING A VIET TABLE

Vietnamese food is the product of an amalgam of cultures, so there's flexibility when setting a table. Before a Vietnamese meal, my husband asks, "What do we need to eat with?" Together we inventory the menu to determine what's required. For traditional Vietnamese menus (a soup, vegetable, main dish, and rice), we set out a salad-size plate and a rice bowl for each person; if needed, we'll include a small dipping-sauce dish too. If there's no soup that day, we may just eat on dinner plates. If bulky foods or entrees that require wrapping are involved, we use dinner plates; when placed under big bowls of noodle soup, they can serve as handsome chargers and are useful for holding spent herb sprigs, lime wedges, and the like (or, we set out a communal plate for refuse).

Chopsticks are the primary Viet eating utensils. Along with China, Japan, and Korea, Vietnam is an official chopstick-wielding county. Place a pair, along with a Chinese or Western soupspoon, on the right side of each plate. Add a knife and fork if the menu requires them. If you or your fellow diners are not comfortable using chopsticks, add forks and spoons. If it's a DIY, hands-on meal, keep paper towels handy.

Other essentials

COCONUT MILK

Buy full-fat unsweetened coconut milk. The degree of richness varies among brands, so check the label. Super-rich Chaokoh has 14 grams of fat per ⅓-cup serving. It's akin to heavy cream.

> BRANDS / Chaokoh, Thai Kitchen, Trader Joe's (less fat but bright, fresh flavor), 365 Everyday Value (Whole Foods brand)

COCONUT OIL

Select virgin, or "unrefined," coconut oil for bold flavor and alluring fragrance. The jars are typically shelved in the regular oil section.

> BRANDS / Dr. Bronner's, Nutiva, Spectrum

COCONUT WATER

As with wine, cook with coconut water that you like to drink! The various brands vary in flavor, depending on where the coconuts came from (Southeast Asian coconuts yield great water) and how the water was processed. Some are bright and sweet, while others are delicate and mild. Check the nutrition label for the sugar amount (it's typically 10 to 14 grams per 8-fluid-ounce serving) to gauge how the water will taste and impact your food. Coconut water is mostly shelved with juices.

> BRANDS / Harmless Harvest, Taste Nirvana, 365 Everyday Value (Whole Foods brand)

DRIED SHIITAKE MUSHROOM

The dried shiitake mushrooms at American supermarkets are delicate and thin. They rehydrate after soaking in hot water for 15 minutes (very handy), but they lack the deep flavor of the thicker ones sold at Asian markets, which may be simply labeled "Dried Mushroom." I used the thinner mushrooms for the recipes in this book. If you do use dried shiitakes from an Asian market, soak them longer (even overnight). You may also need to slice them thinner or chop them smaller. Gently squeeze rehydrated shiitakes to expel excess moisture, then stem and prep as needed.

> BRANDS / Dynasty, Orchid

FRIED ONIONS

Fried onions, the crispy kind commonly used at Thanksgiving for green bean casseroles, are a convenient stand-in for fried shallots, which many modern Viet cooks buy at Chinese and Southeast Asian markets. The fried bits are a fun, fatty garnish. If you don't have some handy, your Viet dish won't be ruined.

BRANDS / French's, Trader Joe's (holiday season only)

RICE CRACKERS

Round and as big as vinyl records, toasted Vietnamese rice crackers (*bánh đa* and *bánh tráng nướng*) are often broken into small pieces and employed like croutons or used to scoop up salads and other piquant mixtures. Good options are hard to find outside of Little Saigon grocers and delis, but you'll be fine with the small toasted rice crackers from the supermarket. Lightly salted ones, with or without sesame seeds, are great, but those with fancy flavors do not work well with Viet food.

BRANDS / Ka-me, Trader Joe's

TOFU

Look for tofu in the produce department or near the dairy case. (Wonton and other dumpling wrappers are usually there too.) Here, you'll be using silken (sold in tubs), firm and extra-firm (one or two blocks in each water-packed tub), and super-firm (in vacuum-sealed packages with minimal water visible). Package weights vary by brand, which is why I often give a range in my ingredients lists. And for these recipes, there's no need to press or weight down tofu to drain it of moisture. Just pour the water out of the tub and prep as directed. A market's own brand of tofu is often good.

BRANDS / Nasoya, O Organics (Albertsons brand), Trader Joe's, Wildwood, 365 Everyday Value (Whole Foods brand)

1

Build your foundation for making great Vietnamese food with this collection of fundamental recipes. The blueprints for serving lettuce and fresh herbs and for making rice paper rolls will further enhance your Viet food adventure.

BASIC RECIPES
and know-how

PERFECT rice

**MAKES ABOUT 4½ CUPS,
TO SERVE 4**

TAKES 40 MINUTES

1½ cups long-grain rice,
  preferably white jasmine

1¾ cups plus 2 tablespoons
  water

Fluffy grains of rice are essential to everyday Vietnamese eating, which is why rice was the first thing I learned to cook. You can prepare it in an electric rice cooker, a pressure cooker, or a multi-cooker, but you're not going to get consistently good results or be able to troubleshoot unless you've practiced cooking rice in a pot on the stove top. Some people boil and drain rice like pasta, but to best express the grain's flavor and texture, I stick with an easy, old-fashioned approach that involves a heavy saucepan and a gradual lowering of the heat. Make rice in the same pan on a regular basis, and soon, you'll be eyeballing the level of the water instead of measuring it.

Long-grain rice is the default for most Vietnamese meals, and white jasmine rice is the go-to, but people are increasingly choosing healthier, fast-cooking brown jasmine rice (see page 14 for a buying guide). For tender-chewy long-grain rice, I rebel against package directions suggesting 1½ to 2 cups of water for 1 cup of rice. The mushy results don't work with Viet food. Instead, I opt for 1¼ cups of water per 1 cup of rice (a 5:4 ratio). It's easier to add water to the pot than to remove it. To get a clean, fresh flavor, wash and rinse the rice before cooking.

/

Put the rice in a medium saucepan and add water to cover by about 1 inch. Swish with your fingers to loosen surface starch. Pour off the water and repeat two or three times, or until the water is nearly clear (it will never be crystal clear). Dump the rice into a mesh strainer, shake to expel excess water, and return the rice to the pan.

Add the 1¾ cups plus 2 tablespoons water to the pan and bring to a boil over high heat, stirring occasionally to prevent clumping. Lower the heat slightly and let simmer briskly for 1 to 3 minutes, stirring occasionally, until glossy on top. A few craters may form, which is fine. Turn the heat to low, cover the pan, and cook for 10 minutes.

Turn off the heat and let the rice sit for 10 minutes. Uncover, fluff with chopsticks or a fork to circulate the grains, re-cover, and let rest again for 10 minutes to complete cooking. The rice will stay warm, covered, for 30 minutes. Fluff once more before serving.

Rice triples in volume during cooking, so adjust the pan size when scaling this recipe up or down. Use the examples in the following chart.

LONG-GRAIN RICE	WATER	SAUCEPAN	YIELD
1 cup	1¼ cups	1½- to 2-quart	3 cups; 2 or 3 servings
2 cups	2½ cups	2- to 3-quart	6 cups; 4 to 6 servings

If your cooked rice is too dry, sprinkle on some water, cover, and warm on low heat for 10 minutes to hydrate; then fluff. If the rice is mushy, when you make your next batch, decrease the water by 1 tablespoon per 1 cup of rice. Tinker to find the best ratio of water to rice for you.

Leftover rice keeps well in the fridge for up to 5 days. Make a large batch and reheat in the microwave, sprinkled with a little water and covered with parchment or wax paper.

To prepare Thai-grown brown jasmine rice, use a 3:4 ratio of rice to water. Wash and rinse 1½ cups brown jasmine rice and return the rice to the pan. (The bran is intact, so one rinse will do; don't expect any starch to be released.) Add 2 cups water, bring to a boil, and then lower the heat to medium. Simmer briskly, partially covered, for about 5 minutes, stirring occasionally, until the liquid is opaque light beige and slightly thick. Turn the heat to low, cover completely, and cook for 20 minutes. The rest remains the same. Let sit, fluff, and let rest as directed.

When making **rice for fried rice**, turn the cooked rice onto a rimmed baking sheet, spreading it out to allow the grains to dry quickly so they will fry up nicely. Let cool completely, uncovered, 1 to 2 hours, before frying. Or, cover the baking sheet with plastic wrap and refrigerate overnight.

ANY DAY viet pickle

MAKES ABOUT 3 CUPS

**TAKES 10 TO 30 MINUTES,
PLUS 1 HOUR TO MATURE**

One 1-pound daikon, or two
8-ounce purple-top turnips
or watermelon radishes

One 6-ounce carrot

1 teaspoon fine sea salt

2 teaspoons sugar,
plus ½ cup

1¼ cups distilled white
vinegar (preferably Heinz)

1 cup lukewarm water

Keep this flash pickle around to add color, crunch, and tang to Vietnamese dishes. Simply called *đồ chua* ("sour stuff"), the daikon and carrot pickle is a banh mi must-have and a perfect side for rice plates and grilled meats. You can substitute turnips or watermelon radish for the daikon; the Notes have more ideas. If the pickle turns stinky as it ages, open the jar and let it air out for 15 minutes before using.

/

Peel and cut the daikon into sticks about 3 inches long and ¼ inch thick (the width of an average chopstick). Peel and cut the carrot into sticks a little skinnier than the daikon.

Put both vegetables in a bowl and toss with the salt and 2 teaspoons sugar. Massage and knead for 3 minutes, or set aside for 20 minutes, until you can bend a piece of daikon so the tips touch without breaking. They will have lost about a quarter of their original volume.

Rinse the vegetables with water, drain in a mesh strainer or colander, and press or shake to expel excess water. Transfer to a 4-cup jar.

In a medium bowl, stir together the remaining ½ cup sugar with the vinegar and 1 cup water until dissolved. Pour enough of the liquid into the jar to cover the vegetables, discard any excess, and let sit for 1 hour. Use immediately, or refrigerate for up to 1 month.

NOTES /

Instead of daikon, use 12 ounces of red radishes. Cut them, unpeeled, into ⅛-inch-thick rounds. Halve the carrot lengthwise, and thinly slice on the diagonal to coax faster pickling. Toss the vegetables in the salt and sugar, let sit for 10 minutes to soften, then rinse and brine as directed.

Don't like daikon funk? Pickle a 10-ounce package of shredded carrot. Enjoy as is, or mix with sliced green cabbage in a 1:2 ratio of carrot to cabbage, add some of the brine, and season with salt. Let sit for 10 minutes to slightly wilt the cabbage and yield a slaw-like mixture to pair with Viet foods.

NUOC CHAM dipping sauce

MAKES ABOUT 1 CUP

TAKES 10 MINUTES

2 to 2½ tablespoons sugar, or 3 to 4 tablespoons maple syrup

3 to 4 tablespoons fresh lime juice

½ cup warm water, or as needed

2 teaspoons unseasoned Japanese rice vinegar (optional)

3 to 4 tablespoons fish sauce

OPTIONAL ADD-INS

1 or 2 Thai or serrano chiles, thinly sliced (keep seeds intact); or 2 to 3 teaspoons chile garlic sauce (see facing page) or sambal oelek

1 large garlic clove, minced

½ small carrot, cut into thin matchsticks or coarsely grated

I've been making Vietnam's ubiquitous *nước chấm* for decades but still prepare it in stages to dial in the flavor. Much like making a vinaigrette, taste, taste, taste. Follow this recipe, then create your own formula. With the optional additions, choose chile for heat, garlic for pungency, and/or carrot for texture.

/

In a small bowl, combine 2 tablespoons of the sugar (or 3 tablespoons of the maple syrup), 3 tablespoons of the lime juice, and the water. Taste the limeade and, if needed, add the remaining 1½ teaspoons sugar (or 1 tablespoon maple syrup) and/or 1 tablespoon lime juice; dilute with water if you go too far. If there's an unpleasant tart-bitter edge, add the vinegar to fix the flavor.

Add the fish sauce to the bowl; how much you use depends on the brand and your own taste. Aim for a bold, forward finish that's a little gutsy. (Keep in mind that this sauce typically dresses dishes that include unsalted ingredients such as lettuce and herbs, which will need an extra flavor lift.) If desired, add the chiles, garlic, and/or carrot. (Offer the chiles on the side if diners are sensitive to their heat.) The sauce can sit at room temperature for up to 8 hours until serving.

Set the sauce at the table so diners may help themselves, or portion it out in small bowls in advance of serving.

NOTES /

Lime juice dulls and can turn the sauce slightly bitter when left overnight. For a **make-ahead nước chấm**, combine the sugar, water, and fish sauce to create a base, then refrigerate for up to 2 weeks. (Prep a double batch if you use it a lot.) To finish, add the lime juice, vinegar (if using), and any desired add-ins.

For a **vegetarian nước chấm**, stir together a rounded ½ teaspoon fine sea salt, 3 tablespoons packed light brown sugar (or 4 to 5 tablespoons maple syrup), and 3 tablespoons lime juice. Taste and add sweetener or up to 1 teaspoon unseasoned Japanese rice vinegar to round out. Add ⅔ cup lukewarm water and 1½ teaspoons soy sauce and finish with any add-ins before serving.

CHILE GARLIC sauce

MAKES ABOUT ⅔ CUP

TAKES 10 MINUTES, PLUS
30 MINUTES TO REST

6 ounces hot or medium-hot
red chiles, such as Fresno,
jalapeño, or serrano,
coarsely chopped, with
seeds intact

4 garlic cloves, coarsely
chopped

Fine sea salt

1 tablespoon sugar,
plus more as needed

1½ tablespoons distilled
white vinegar (preferably
Heinz), plus more as
needed

In the late summer and early fall, when chiles are at their plump, red-hot best, I load up to make this condiment. It's my version of *tương ớt tỏi Việt-Nam*, the chile garlic sauce that Huy Fong (the "rooster brand") developed for the Viet palate. The commercial product is sold at supermarkets in plastic jars next to its Indonesian kin, sambal oelek. But when made at home, chile garlic sauce is brighter tasting, and you can play with the heat, sweetness, and tang. It's super-simple and fast to make, with a payoff that lasts for months.

/

In a food processor, combine the chiles, garlic, ½ teaspoon salt, sugar, and vinegar and whirl to a coarse texture. Take a whiff; it should make you sweat a bit.

Transfer the chile mixture to a small saucepan. Bring to a gentle simmer over medium heat, then lower the heat and continue simmering softy for about 3 minutes, or until the sauce no longer smells raw.

Remove the pan from the heat and set aside to cool for 5 minutes. Season with salt, a pinch at a time, to add savory depth, and sweeten with more sugar, ½ teaspoon at a time, to curb the heat. Add more vinegar, ½ to 1 teaspoon at a time, to brighten. Aim for a spicy, slightly sweet, tangy finish. Let it rest, uncovered, for about 30 minutes to cool, mellow, and mature before using. The sauce may be stored in an airtight container, refrigerated, for up to 6 months.

HOW TO CHOP CHILES WITHOUT GLOVES

When working with hot chiles, I don't wear gloves to protect my hands from their fiery oils. Instead, I minimize contact by using the stem of the chile as my helper.

To chop a chile, quarter it lengthwise but keep the stem intact. Hold on to the stem while cutting the chile crosswise; if needed, chop further. Then use the stem to scoot the chile pieces onto the side of your knife blade and use the stem again to push off the chile pieces into a bowl or wherever they are needed. If you mistakenly touch the seeds or inner membranes, promptly wash your hands with coarse salt and soap.

CARAMEL sauce

MAKES ABOUT ½ CUP

TAKES 15 MINUTES

2 tablespoons water,
   plus ¼ cup

⅛ teaspoon unseasoned
   rice, apple, or distilled
   white vinegar (optional)

½ cup cane sugar

This key Viet ingredient is simply nearly burnt sugar; it's not at all the caramel sauce for topping ice cream. Vietnamese caramel sauce is stealthily employed in savory dishes to impart a lovely mahogany color and build savory-sweet depth. You've likely had caramel sauce in clay-pot (*kho*) dishes but didn't know it. Like molasses, it can be added to grilled-meat marinades to enhance the appearance of the final dish.

Don't fear the caramelization process. It's not overly dramatic, and the vinegar prevents crystallization, which can result in crusty failed batches. (If you wish, use strained fresh lemon or lime juice in place of vinegar.) Employ cane sugar, such as C&H brand, because it caramelizes consistently better than beet sugar. The result is an inky, bittersweet Vietnamese staple. I keep a jar of caramel sauce to cut down on prep work. If you don't have time to make a batch, use the work-arounds in the recipes to make some on the spot. Select a small, heavy-bottomed saucepan with a long handle and a light interior (such as stainless steel) to observe the caramelization.

/

Fill the sink (or a large bowl or pot) with enough water to come halfway up the sides of the saucepan.

In the saucepan, combine the 2 tablespoons water, vinegar (if using), and sugar. Set over medium heat and cook, stirring with a heat-proof spatula or metal spoon; when the sugar has nearly or fully dissolved, stop stirring. Let the sugar syrup bubble vigorously for 5 to 6 minutes, until it takes on the shade of light tea. Turn the heat to medium-low to stabilize the cooking. Turn on the exhaust to vent the inevitable smoke. (Don't worry if sugar crystallizes on the pan wall. But if things get crusty in the bubbling sugar syrup, add another drop of vinegar to correct it.) For even cooking, you may occasionally lift and swirl the saucepan.

Cook the syrup for about 2 minutes longer, until it is the color of dark tea. The next 1 to 2 minutes are critical because the sugar will darken by the second. Monitor the cooking and, to control the caramelization, frequently pick up the saucepan and slowly swirl the syrup. When a dark reddish cast sets in—think the color of Pinot Noir—let the sugar cook a few seconds longer to a color between Cabernet and black coffee. Remove from the heat and place the pan in the water to stop the cooking. Expect the pan bottom to sizzle upon contact.

Leaving the pan in the sink, add the remaining ¼ cup water. The sugar will seize up, which is okay. When the dramatic bubbling reaction stops, return the pan to medium-high heat, and cook briefly, stirring to loosen and dissolve the sugar.

Remove the pan from the heat and return to the water in the sink for about 1 minute, stirring, to stop the cooking process and cool the caramel sauce to room temperature.

Use the sauce immediately, or transfer to a small heatproof glass jar, let cool completely, and then cap and store in a cool, dark place indefinitely.

POMEGRANATE *molasses*

MAKES A SCANT ½ CUP

TAKES 30 MINUTES, PLUS ABOUT 1 HOUR TO COOL

2 cups pomegranate juice

1 tablespoon plus 1 teaspoon strained fresh lemon juice, plus more as needed

¼ cup sugar

Why is this recipe for a Middle Eastern ingredient in a Vietnamese cookbook? Because I needed an accessible substitute for tamarind liquid, a fruity-tart seasoning for southern Vietnamese–style seafood stir-fries and soups. Having spied pomegranates (*lựu*) being sold by Hanoi street vendors in 2015, I pondered its use in Viet cooking. Turns out the Middle Eastern fruit pairs well with fish sauce and other Viet flavors to create newish dishes such as Pomegranate Sriracha Shrimp (page 109) and Tangy Seafood Stew (page 75). If your supermarket doesn't stock pomegranate molasses (check the sweeteners and international foods sections), use this recipe to make it from bottled juice, such as Pom brand. For cooks who want to go old-school, the Notes offer tamarind tips.

/

To make in the microwave In a 4-cup glass measuring cup (or similar microwave-safe container), combine the pomegranate juice, lemon juice, and sugar and microwave on high in 4- to 5-minute intervals, until the mixture has reduced to ½ cup of syrup, 20 to 25 minutes.

To make on the stove top In a 1½- or 2-quart saucepan over high heat, combine the pomegranate juice, lemon juice, and sugar and bring to a boil, stirring occasionally to dissolve the sugar. Turn the heat to medium-high to maintain a vigorous simmer or a low boil and let the liquid bubble for 25 to 30 minutes, swirling the pan now and then for even cooking, until it's reduced by 75 percent; you should have ½ cup of syrup. (The syrup should easily coat the back of a spoon with a thickish cabernet-colored film. If you run your finger through, the line should hold; but be careful, because it's hot.)

Regardless of your cooking method, let the hot syrup cool for 15 minutes, then transfer to a glass jar and let cool completely, uncovered, to further concentrate and thicken. Taste the molasses, and if a tart edge is needed, add more lemon juice, ½ teaspoon at a time, whisking or stirring well to combine.

Store the molasses, refrigerated, for up to 6 months. If it firms up, warm it to liquify before using.

NOTES /

Tamarind is sold at many Chinese, Southeast Asian, South Asian, and Latin markets. Look for double-wrapped dark brown blocks of "seedless pulp" in the spice or seasonings aisle; brittle looking tan-colored pods of sour tamarind may be in the produce section. (Sweet tamarind is a delicious snack but not tangy enough for cooking.)

To make **tamarind liquid** from one 14- to 16-ounce block of seedless pulp, break the block into six chunks, then combine them with 4 cups water in a medium saucepan and simmer for 10 minutes to soften. Turn off the heat and let steep, covered, for 30 minutes. Stir with a fork to break up, then strain through a coarse-mesh sieve, pressing on the solids and scraping off the thick liquid. If needed, return the pulp to the pan, add some of the strained liquid, stir to release more pulp, and then restrain. You'll have about 3 cups.

When available, shell 8 ounces of tamarind pods to net 4 ounces of flesh and seeds. Combine with 1 cup water in a small saucepan and simmer for 2 to 4 minutes, stirring to loosen the flesh. Cover and set aside for 10 minutes, then pass through a coarse-mesh strainer. If you like, combine the seeds with 2 tablespoons recently boiled water, stir, and then harvest more liquid to yield about ⅔ cup.

The liquid may be kept refrigerated for 1 week or frozen up to 6 months (freeze in ice-cube trays and then transfer to an airtight container).

Homemade tamarind liquid has better flavor and texture than store-bought concentrate and paste. When using tamarind to substitute for pomegranate molasses in this book's recipes, apply these conversions.

1 tablespoon pomegranate molasses equals	2 tablespoons homemade tamarind liquid
	1½ teaspoons syrupy tamarind concentrate mixed with 1½ teaspoons water
	2½ to 3 tablespoons tamarind paste, such as Spice Perfection brand

PRESSURE-COOKER chicken stock

MAKES ABOUT 6 CUPS

TAKES ABOUT 1½ HOURS

1½ to 1¾ pounds chicken backs

1 pound meaty chicken parts, such as drumsticks, thighs, or breast

Chubby 1½-inch (1½-ounce) section ginger, unpeeled, cut into 3 pieces and bruised

½ small Fuji apple, peeled, cored, and coarsely chopped

1 medium yellow onion, halved and thickly sliced

1¼ teaspoons fine sea salt

I keep canned chicken broth in my pantry, and I also make my own. The pressure cooker makes excellent stock quickly, but you can take the more traditional route and simmer the stock in a stockpot, which takes longer (see the Notes). Chicken backs alone don't yield super-tasty stock because, although they may be fatty, they aren't meaty enough. Given that, combine the backs (ask for them at the meat counter if you don't keep a frozen stash) with meaty parts like drumsticks, which are often well priced; wings aren't as flavorful. If backs are unavailable, use more meaty parts.

I parboil the parts to remove most of the scum that may cause the stock to taste slightly off; that step does not diminish the flavor. The apple helps to create a savory-sweet edge. Once things get going, gingery and chicken-y aromas will fill your kitchen, and you'll have a rich, viscous stock to enhance your food. Save the harvested fat and pick the meat off the bones if you're making the chicken and celery rice on page 189.

/

Put the chicken backs and parts in a 6-quart pressure cooker with enough water to just cover. Partially cover the pot with the lid (there's no need to lock it in place) and bring to a vigorous simmer over high heat. (If using a multicooker, use a high heat setting, such as Brown on the Fagor Lux, or adjust the Sauté function on the Instant Pot.) Uncover and simmer for 1 to 2 minutes, then turn off the heat.

Set a colander in the sink, dump in the chicken and all the liquid, and quickly rinse and spray off the impurities. Transfer the chicken to a bowl and set aside. Give the pressure cooker a scrubbing and then return the chicken to it. Add 6⅓ cups water to the cooker. (If using a multicooker, add 6 cups water.) Drop in the ginger, apple, onion, and salt.

Lock the lid in place. Bring to high pressure, adjust the heat to maintain pressure, and cook for 45 minutes. Then, remove from the heat, depressurize naturally for 20 minutes, and release the residual pressure. (If using a multicooker, program it to cook at high pressure for 45 minutes, turn it off or unplug it, and depressurize for 25 minutes before releasing residual pressure.)

Unlock the cooker and wait for any bubbling to subside, about 5 minutes. Using a metal ladle, remove most of the fat on top, leaving some for flavor. (Or, remove the fat after straining and chilling the stock, when it's easier.) Using a slotted spoon, remove the large solids.

Position a strainer over a medium or large saucepan (line the strainer with muslin for super-clear stock and easy straining) and ladle or pour the stock through.

Use the stock immediately, or transfer to airtight containers and refrigerate for up to 3 days or freeze for up to 3 months.

NOTES /

When whole chickens are on sale, buy a couple, cut them up (or ask a butcher to do the deed) and use the backs and some of the meaty parts for stock. Add 3 or 4 chicken feet for extra-gelatinous stock.

To make the stock in a 6-quart stockpot, parboil the chicken as directed. Return the chicken to the cleaned pot and add 8 cups water with the onion, ginger, and salt. Bring to a gentle simmer and continue simmering, uncovered, for 2 hours. Remove from the heat and let cool and rest for 15 minutes before straining. If needed, boil to reduce to about 6 cups, or add water if the stock is too strong.

THE DIFFERENCE BETWEEN "BRUISE" AND "SMASH"

When you want to unleash the power of an aromatic, such as garlic, ginger, or lemongrass, you need to bruise or smash it. What's the difference? A *bruise* partially crushes a relatively thick ingredient to initiate its flavor release (great for stews, braises, and stocks); the ingredient remains intact and is easy to later retrieve from the pot. A more powerful *smash* crushes and flattens an ingredient to quickly unlock it flavors (ideal for stir-fries and sauces that get strained). Use a meat mallet, heavy saucepan, or flat side of a knife to do either; your tool depends on the thickness and density of the ingredient.

PRESSURE-COOKER vegetable stock

MAKES ABOUT 6 CUPS

TAKES 1 HOUR

1 tablespoon canola or other neutral oil

Chubby ¾-inch (¾-ounce) section ginger, unpeeled, cut into 3 or 4 slices

One 8-ounce yellow onion, halved and thickly sliced

One 4-ounce carrot, sliced (scrub and use unpeeled if you like)

One 3-ounce celery stalk, coarsely chopped

4 ounces large white mushrooms, stems included, coarsely chopped

12 ounces napa or green cabbage leaves, coarsely chopped

½ small Fuji apple, peeled, cored, and coarsely chopped (optional)

1½ teaspoons fine sea salt

For excellent Viet dishes that require vegetable stock, make your own. The flavor of commercially sold vegetable stock or broth has been developed for Western dishes. You can use them in a pinch, but homemade stock yields clean, deep flavor. It's easy to prepare and economical too. You can use vegetables that are past their prime. Flabby napa cabbage leaves boost flavor. I freeze asparagus trimmings and toss a handful into the pot to build umami depth. Using weight measurements for the vegetables ensures a good balance of flavors.

Cooking the ginger and onion in oil before adding them to the pot lends the stock additional richness and body. The apple provides sweetness, which slightly offsets the vegetables' mineral qualities.

/

In a 6-quart pressure cooker over medium-high heat, warm the oil, then add the ginger and onion and cook for 1 to 2 minutes, until fragrant. (If using a multicooker, select a high-heat function, such as Brown for the Fagor Lux, or adjust the Sauté function on the Instant Pot.) Add 5⅓ cups water to the cooker. (If using a multicooker, add 5 cups water.) Add the carrot, celery, mushrooms, cabbage, apple (if using), and salt.

Lock the lid in place. Bring to high pressure, adjust the heat to maintain pressure, and cook for 15 minutes. Then, remove from the heat, depressurize naturally for 15 minutes, and release the residual pressure. (If using a multicooker, program it to cook at high pressure for 15 minutes, turn it off or unplug it, and depressurize for 20 minutes before releasing residual pressure.)

Unlock the cooker and wait for any bubbling to subside, about 5 minutes.

Position a muslin-lined strainer over a 2- to 3-quart saucepan and then ladle or pour the stock through. Let cool briefly, then press or twist the fabric to get more stock from the solids.

Use the stock immediately, or transfer to airtight containers and refrigerate for up to 3 days or freeze for up to 3 months.

If you don't have muslin for straining the stock, use a nut milk bag or a super-fine strainer.

If your yield is a little shy, add about ½ cup water to the vegetable solids and wring them out again in the muslin to obtain additional liquid. Sometimes they need a little help.

To make the stock in a 6-quart stockpot, combine the sautéed ginger and onion, 6¾ cups water, and the remaining vegetables, apple, and salt. Bring to a gentle simmer and continue simmering, uncovered, for 1 hour. Then, remove from the heat and let cool for 15 minutes. Strain the stock, squeezing the solids. If needed, boil to reduce to 6 cups; or add water if you have less and the stock is too strong.

WHY MUSLIN IS THE BETTER CHEESECLOTH

Available at fabric stores, muslin is affordable, machine washable, and reusable. It's terrific for straining stocks and soup broths, catching impurities like a dream. I've also used it to efficiently expel moisture from zucchini and tofu, strain yogurt, and in other cooking tasks. Look for lightweight muslin suitable for lining quilts. Tear it into 18-inch squares and wash with fragrance-free soap before the first use. After using, rinse the muslin well and wash again.

lettuce-and-herb cheat sheet

You don't need a recipe for the platter of leafy garnishes that go with many Viet dishes. Its purposes are to:

Provide pieces of soft leafy greens that can be used to encase food or commingle well with other ingredients. Choose leaf lettuce, such as butter, Boston, or red or green leaf, that can bend and fold. Mild mustard greens and radicchio add a spicy bite. Heirloom lettuces make a beautiful presentation. Baby lettuce mixes are great for rice paper rolls and rice noodle bowls. For lettuce wraps, serve whole leaves for diners to tear into palm-size pieces, or precut the lettuce.

Inject herbaceous notes. Start with pungent cilantro and zingy mint, the foundational herbs in the Viet kitchen. They're easy to buy and grow. Try other herbs too, such as basil (Italian, Thai, lemon, lime, or opal, for example) or dill. Like a Viet cook, experiment with what's fresh and in season.

Create a personalized eating experience. The lettuce and herbs allow diners to fashion their own textures, flavors, and colors with each mouthful. Feel free to tinker. For example, to add refreshing crunch, include sliced cucumber or the daikon and carrot pickle on page 29.

When dealing with the nitty-gritty details, keep in mind the following things to establish your own approach.

How much to serve: This book's recipes suggest quantities for four moderate eaters. Once you get the hang of eating this way, you'll know how much to offer.

Advance prep options: Prewash and spin lettuce and herbs so they're ready when you are. See page 19 for tips.

How to display: Consider potential traffic jams at the table. When serving four people, arrange the lettuce and herbs on one large platter, if it's reachable by everyone from their seats, or two dinner plates to be shared by pairs of diners. Have one or two sets of other garnishes as needed. Table setting tips are on page 21.

How to assemble lettuce wraps: Take a sprig or two of herb plus a piece or whole lettuce leaf. If it's a giant, unwieldy leaf, tear it into a palm-size piece; if the leaf's spine comes off, set it aside. Cilantro sprigs may be torn into shorter lengths. Pinch off mint or basil leaves from their stems. I usually layer on the main feature (protein and maybe noodles), herbs, and any other garnishes on the leaf. Then, I fold and bundle up the lettuce, dunk into dipping sauce, eat, and repeat.

rice paper rolls 101

All Vietnamese rice paper rolls follow the same drill: Moisten the rice paper, wait for it to soften and get tacky, fill it, and then roll it up. Use this blueprint for your adventures.

Pre-roll, or roll your own. Finished rolls are great for a cocktail party or buffet. But for a fun meal with lots of group participation, lay out the components and let diners make their own.

Filling rules. Practically anything can go into a rice paper roll, so long as it's soft or thin. The filling should be easily manipulated and contained. To prepare the filling, remove lettuce spines or cut leaves into ribbons (use baby lettuce mix as is). Chop or tear herbs to prevent awkward eating moments. Cut ingredients into matchsticks or slice them, as needed.

Rice paper roll setup. Whether making the rolls in the kitchen or at the table, ready these items:

- For a work surface when making the rolls in the kitchen, use a cutting board, inverted baking sheet, or non-terry dish towel. When it's a DIY situation, provide a dinner plate for each diner.

- To moisten the rice papers, have a large, deep skillet or shallow bowl (something that's wider than the rice paper) filled with 1 to 2 inches of very warm water (a little hotter than bathwater, since it will cool as you work). When making rolls at the table, set out two communal dipping vessels.

- Arrange the filling components (lettuce, herbs, noodles, proteins) near your work area in the kitchen or on the table. If people are eating as they roll, ready the sauce too.

How to Make Rice Paper Rolls

1. Slide a rice paper into the water and rotate for a few seconds to wet both sides, then place on your work surface. *Do not* soak the rice paper or leave it sitting in water because it will oversoak, become unmanageable, and maybe fall apart.

2. Wait about 1 minute for the rice paper to become pliable and tacky (like a sticky note), then start layering the filling in the lower third of the rice paper. Lettuce usually goes down first as a foundation. The rest is up to you.

3. Bring up the bottom edge of the rice paper to cover the filling. Then, roll away from you once; the lettuce now faces you and the rice paper edge is tucked under. With the filling held in place, you can more easily manipulate the rolling process.

4. To create an optional peekaboo effect, place a few pieces of filling snugly along the partially finished roll. Once the roll is done, those final additions show through the last layer of rice paper.

5. Fold in the side flaps to cover the filling. (If things look too full, fold in one side and let stuff spill out the other end.) Finish rolling, jelly roll–style, to create a small burrito-like package. The rice paper is self-sealing, and now ready to eat or store.

Shelf life and advance prep. To hold or transport to a party, weave plastic wrap between the rolls (to prevent sticking) or arrange in a circle (like daisy petals) with corners barely touching. Cover with plastic wrap and keep at moderate room temperature for up to 3 hours. (Refrigerated rolls harden and may come apart if the filling is wet.)

2

Bake, scoop, wrap, and roll your way to a wide variety of thrilling Vietnamese snacks and small bites. Don't overlook the bonus riffs and ideas in the recipe Notes.

snacks

CHILE GARLIC chicken wings

SERVES 6 TO 8

TAKES 1 HOUR

Canola spray oil

2 pounds chicken drumettes and flats ("party wings"; 16 to 20 pieces)

½ cup all-purpose flour or rice flour (white or brown, such as Bob's Red Mill)

½ teaspoon fine sea salt

½ teaspoon recently ground black pepper

1 tablespoon paprika

1 tablespoon sugar

1½ tablespoons fish sauce

2 to 3 tablespoons chile garlic sauce (see page 31; use the maximum if homemade)

¼ cup light corn syrup or brown rice syrup (such as Lundberg)

1 Persian or ½ English cucumber, thickly sliced (optional)

1 lime, cut into wedges (optional)

Nibbling on chicken wings with an ice-cold beer is a great way to nosh Vietnamese style, but I don't get out the fryer to make the wings. Instead, I coat them in flour, spices, and oil and roast them. Remarkably, they crisp up as if you'd deep-fried them. Rice flour yields slightly crisper results than wheat flour, but it's a marginal difference so use what you like. If you don't have cooking spray or a hand-pump oil mister, oil the foil and then tumble the flour-coated wings in 2 to 3 tablespoons of neutral oil before roasting.

For a party, roast the wings in advance, cover loosely, and keep at a cool room temperature for up to 2 hours. When you're ready to serve, reheat in a 350°F oven for 6 minutes, until hot, and then toss with the sauce. Sauced wings keep their texture well for about 1 hour.

/

Preheat the oven to 425°F. Line a rimmed baking sheet with aluminum foil and coat with cooking spray. Pat the wings dry with paper towels.

In a large bowl, combine the flour, salt, pepper, and paprika. Add all the chicken and toss, using your hands to ensure a thorough coating. Transfer to the prepared baking sheet. Spray the chicken on both sides with oil, then spread out the wings on the pan for even cooking.

Roast the wings for 45 minutes, turning after 30 minutes, or when they hiss and are browned on the underside. The magic happens in the last 15 minutes, when they become richly browned and crispy.

While the wings roast, in a small saucepan over medium heat, combine the sugar, fish sauce, chile garlic sauce, and corn syrup and bring to a boil. Let bubble vigorously for 45 to 60 seconds, until thick (look for biggish bubbles on the surface). Set aside to cool for a few minutes, then transfer to a large bowl to finish cooling and thickening, about 15 minutes.

When the wings are done, let them rest for about 5 minutes, then toss in the sauce and transfer to a platter.

Serve the wings with the cucumber slices on the side, if desired, for a cooling crunch. Have diners add a squeeze of lime juice for bright contrast, if they like.

ROASTED CAULIFLOWER *"wings"*

SERVES 4 TO 6

TAKES 1 HOUR

1 to 1¼ pounds cauliflower florets

5⅝ ounces white or brown rice flour (such as Bob's Red Mill)

1 teaspoon fine sea salt

¼ to ½ teaspoon recently ground black pepper (use the maximum for a lick of heat)

1¼ teaspoons paprika

Brimming ⅔ cup water

2½ tablespoons canola or other neutral oil

1 tablespoon sugar

1 tablespoon Bragg Liquid Aminos, Maggi Seasoning sauce, or soy sauce

3 tablespoons chile garlic sauce (see page 31)

¼ cup light corn syrup or brown rice syrup (such as Lundberg)

If it's Meatless Monday and I want wings, I coat snack-size cauliflower florets in batter and bake them until crisp on the outside and tender on the inside. As shown on page 46, serving the sauce on the side preserves the just-baked texture well. The batter is a bit tricky, so weigh the flour for an exact measurement.

/

Preheat the oven to 425°F. Line a rimmed baking sheet with parchment paper and coat with neutral oil or cooking spray.

Pat the cauliflower florets dry with paper towels and, if needed, cut into pieces no larger than 2 inches at their widest point. Set aside.

In a large bowl, combine the rice flour, salt, pepper, and paprika. Whisk in the water to hydrate, then add the canola oil; aim for a thick consistency (imagine very soft frosting) that will stick on the cauliflower and bake into a shell-like coating. (If the batter is too thick, whisk in more water, 1 teaspoon at a time; brown rice flour will need an additional 2 to 3 teaspoons.) An overly pasty batter bakes up extra crunchy, but that's not a bad thing.

Add the cauliflower to the batter, using a spatula to coat nearly all exposed surfaces of the florets (a few bare spots are great for ventilation and help to create a crisp finish). Stir and fold the ingredients, turning and shaking the bowl, if it helps. Spread out the florets on the prepared pan, cut-side down, with none touching.

Roast the cauliflower for 30 minutes, until the tops feel dry-ish and hard and the bottoms have browned here and there. Turn the florets and roast 12 to 15 minutes longer to crisp the other side.

Meanwhile, in a small saucepan, stir together the sugar, Bragg Liquid Aminos, chile garlic sauce, and corn syrup. Bring to a brisk simmer over medium heat. Remove from the heat and, after the bubbling action subsides, pour into a small, heatproof bowl. Let cool and thicken for 20 minutes while the cauliflower roasts.

When the cauliflower is done, let cool for 5 to 10 minutes. Serve with the sauce for dipping. Baked florets will remain crisp for 2 hours and can be reheated in a 350°F oven for 5 to 6 minutes, until warm.

SPICY CLAM AND *herb scoops*

SERVES 4

TAKES 25 MINUTES

One 10-ounce can, or two
  6½-ounce cans baby clams
  or chopped clams

2 teaspoons fish sauce,
  plus more as needed

1½ tablespoons canola or
  other neutral oil

3 large white mushrooms,
  stems included, chopped
  into pea-size pieces

2 garlic cloves, finely chopped

2 tablespoons finely chopped
  fresh lemongrass, or
  1½ tablespoon grated
  fresh lemongrass (from
  1 medium stalk)

Scant ¼ teaspoon paprika

⅛ teaspoon cayenne pepper

⅛ teaspoon recently ground
  black or white pepper

⅓ cup thinly sliced
  green onions, white
  and green parts

¼ cup unsalted roasted
  peanuts, coarsely chopped

½ cup lightly packed
  coarsely chopped fresh
  cilantro or mint

1 lime, cut into wedges

Sesame or plain rice
  crackers or tortilla chips
  for serving

When Vietnamese people eat crackers or chips, they often use them like utensils to scoop up crazy-delicious mixtures like this one, called *hến xào xúc bánh đa* in Hue, where it's a favorite. Cooks in Vietnam use mild-tasting tiny fresh clams, and break up large rice crackers into shards for scooping. To replicate the dish with ease, I use canned clams (such as Bar Harbor and Crown Prince) and store-bought lightly salted crackers or chips. Chopped mushrooms make the clams go farther, while adding umami. Cilantro-like Vietnamese coriander (*rau răm*) is the go-to herb, but cilantro or mint work just fine at delivering the flavors of Vietnam. This fun snack is perfect with drinks.

/

Drain the clams, reserving 2 tablespoons of the liquid (save the rest for soup or another use). Season the clams with the fish sauce to add extra ocean flavor. Set aside.

In a medium skillet over medium-high heat, warm 1½ teaspoons of the canola oil, then add the mushrooms and clam liquid. Cook for 2 to 3 minutes, until the liquid has evaporated and the mushrooms have patches of golden brown. Lower the heat slightly and add the remaining 1 tablespoon oil, the garlic, lemongrass, paprika, and cayenne. Cook for about 1 minute, until fragrant, then add the clams. Cook the clams, stirring, for about 2 minutes, until just a little clam liquid remains.

Remove the skillet from the heat and stir in the black pepper and green onions. Let cool at room temperature for 8 to 10 minutes (or cover and leave for up to 2 hours). Add the peanuts and cilantro. For brightness, squeeze the juice from a lime wedge onto the mixture; if savoriness is needed, add a sprinkle of fish sauce and then stir to combine.

Mound the clams on a plate or in a shallow bowl and serve with the remaining lime wedges and the crackers on the side.

HOW TO NAVIGATE CHILE HEAT

Sometimes a jalapeño tastes like a bell pepper, probably because of weather conditions and not your palate. When chiles grow in chilly temperatures, they have less oomph. In that case, just add extra to your food. During hotter months, when the chile heat is on, consider cutting back on the chiles in your recipe but also think about stocking up (see page 18 for freezing tips)! Regardless of the chile variety, the flesh closer to the stem is hotter, as a chile's punch is mostly contained in the capsaicin glands (fleshy membranes) attached to the seeds. To remove seeds but retain heat, use the tip of a knife to gently scrape the seeds out.

STREETSIDE CORN AND chile

SERVES 4

TAKES 15 MINUTES

1½ tablespoons unsalted
butter or virgin coconut oil

2 cups fresh corn kernels

1 seeded and chopped
fresh chile, such as Fresno
or jalapeño

2½ teaspoons fish sauce, or
1½ teaspoons Bragg Liquid
Aminos or Maggi Seasoning
sauce plus ¼ teaspoon
fine sea salt

Rounded ¼ teaspoon
smoked paprika

1 green onion, white and
green parts, thinly sliced
and separated into rings

1½ teaspoons furikake;
3 pieces Korean toasted
seaweed, crumbled; or
½ sheet sushi nori, toasted
and crumbled

Even though corn is a New World food, it is beloved in Vietnam.
There it is often spotlighted in velvety soups, or grilled and coated
with rich green onions and oil (see page 119). But one of the best
ways to eat it is as a spoon-able street food called *bắp xào*: corn
kernels stir-fried in butter with chiles and tiny dried shrimp. It's
a Viet version of *esquites* (Mexican corn salad), and it's super-easy.

For smoky heat, I combine fresh chile with Spanish smoked paprika,
which is sold in the spice aisle. Since dried shrimp is hard to find
at supermarkets, I work in oceanic oomph via Japanese or Korean
toasted seaweed, or Japanese *furikake*, a rice seasoning mixture that
often includes dried bonito.

/

In a large skillet over medium-high heat, melt the butter. Add the
corn and chile and cook for about 2 minutes, until heated through.
Add the fish sauce and smoked paprika and cook, stirring frequently,
for 1 to 2 minutes longer, until the corn has cooked through and
developed a spicy and savory flavor. (In my carbon-steel skillet,
when a couple of kernels jump and pop, it's time to move on.)

Remove the pan from the heat, add the green onion, and stir until
softened. Let cool for 3 to 5 minutes, then transfer to a bowl and top
with the furikake.

Serve with spoons for each diner to mix things up, scoop, and eat.

NOTES /

Buy 3 medium or 2 large ears of corn to obtain 2 cups of kernels. When fresh
chile isn't handy, substitute a rounded ¼ teaspoon cayenne pepper and boost
the smoked paprika to ½ teaspoon.

When prepping the corn, it's safer and less messy to lay the ear on the cutting
board to cut off the kernels, instead of holding the ear upright. But if you prefer,
stand it up with the sturdier stem end down.

MUSHROOM pâté puffs

MAKES ABOUT 30 PUFFS,
TO SERVE 8 TO 10

TAKES ABOUT 1¼ HOURS

3 large dried shiitake
mushrooms, soaked
in ½ cup hot water
for 15 minutes and
strained, reserving
the soaking liquid

2 tablespoons butter or
olive oil

¼ cup finely chopped shallot
or yellow onion

10 ounces fresh white
mushrooms, finely chopped
and including stems

Brimming ¼ teaspoon fine
sea salt

⅛ teaspoon recently ground
black pepper

⅛ teaspoon dried thyme
leaves, or ½ teaspoon fresh
thyme leaves (optional)

Rounded 1½ teaspoons
cornstarch

1 large garlic clove, put
through a press or minced
and mashed

One 7-ounce sheet frozen
puff pastry (such as
Pepperidge Farm), thawed
as directed on the package

1 egg, beaten, or
1½ tablespoons whole milk
or unsweetened soy milk

The French brought *bánh pa-tê sô* (from *pâté chaud*, "hot pastry pie," a nineteenth-century French term) to Vietnam, where people went nuts for them. The dome-shaped savory hand pies are a country-style pâté or a meat loaf–like mixture encased in puff pastry. They were among my favorite childhood breakfast treats.

Since I can rarely afford those kinds of morning calories or the time to make from-scratch dough, I use puff pastry to make *bánh pa-tê sô* into diamond-shaped two-bite snacks. (Bonus: The result has a higher filling-to-pastry ratio than the classic!) Soak the mushrooms overnight for a deeper flavor. These puffs are simple to assemble, so double the recipe and freeze half.

/

Discard the shiitake mushroom stems and finely chop the caps to yield about ¼ cup.

In a medium skillet over medium heat, melt the butter (or warm the olive oil). Add the shallot and cook, stirring occasionally for 3 to 4 minutes, until it begins to brown. Add the shiitake and white mushrooms, 2 tablespoons of the shiitake soaking liquid, the salt, pepper, and thyme (if using). Turn the heat to high and cook, stirring frequently, for about 8 minutes, until reduced to half the original volume. If the mushrooms brown a little, that is okay.

Meanwhile, in a small bowl, mix the cornstarch with 1½ teaspoons of the shiitake soaking liquid.

Turn down the heat to medium to steady the cooking and then add the garlic and cornstarch slurry to the pan. Cook for 45 seconds to bind and firm up the filling, then remove from the heat. Let cool to room temperature, or you can let it get cold. To quickly cool, spread out on a plate or small baking sheet and freeze for 15 minutes, stirring midway through. You should have a scant 1 cup.

Preheat the oven to 400°F. Line a baking sheet with parchment paper.

53
SNACKS

Unfold the pastry and cut it crosswise into three strips, each about 3¼ inches wide (if needed, roll out the pastry with a rolling pin to get you there). Center one third of the filling on each strip, forming it into a single column from end to end. Lift one dry long edge of each strip up and over the filling. Use a brush or finger to moisten the exposed long edge with water. Flatten the moistened edge with your thumb, then roll the log over that edge to seal. Repeat with the remaining strips and filling.

Transfer the logs to a second baking sheet or a pan and freeze for about 5 minutes, or refrigerate for 20 minutes. You want to firm up the logs to facilitate clean cuts; the puffs will bake better as a result. Then, cut each log on the diagonal at 1-inch intervals (if you cut narrower pieces, they're likely to fall over during baking). Transfer to the prepared baking sheet, seam-side down, spaced 1 inch apart, and brush the tops with the egg.

Bake the pastry for 15 to 20 minutes, until puffed, crisp, and browned (egg wash darkens fastest). Let cool for 5 minutes.

Serve the puffs warm or at room temperature.

NOTES /

Pepperidge Farm brand frozen puff pastry is easy to use and bakes up beautifully. This recipe uses half a package.

Use a full-size food processor to chop the shallot (or onion) and mushrooms. Work with one ingredient at a time, cutting it into blueberry-size pieces before pulsing in the machine.

Make the pâté filling in advance and refrigerate, covered, for up to 3 days.

To freeze the uncut and unbaked logs, wrap them in parchment paper and then plastic wrap. Place on a baking sheet and then in the freezer. When hard, transfer to an airtight container or zipper-top plastic bag. The logs will keep for up to 2 months. When ready to use, partially thaw for 20 minutes and then cut into diamond shapes. Preheat the oven while the pastries continue thawing and then bake as directed.

The baked puffs will keep at room temperature for 4 hours. If you like, reheat in a 350°F oven or toaster oven for 5 minutes.

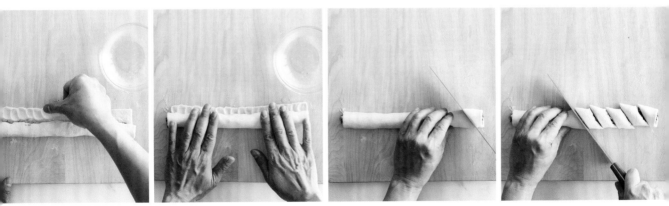

VIETNAMESE empanadas

MAKES 16 EMPANADAS,
TO SERVE 6 TO 8

TAKES ABOUT 1¼ HOURS

1½ tablespoons canola or other neutral oil

3 tablespoons finely chopped shallot or yellow onion

1 large garlic clove, put through a press or minced and mashed

3 ounces ground pork

6 ounces medium shrimp, peeled, deveined, and chopped into pea-size pieces

⅓ cup finely diced jicama or sweet potato

½ teaspoon sugar

¼ teaspoon plus ⅛ teaspoon fine sea salt

Rounded ⅛ teaspoon recently ground black pepper

2 tablespoons chopped green onion, green part only (optional)

1 egg

2 teaspoons water

One 14- or 16-ounce box refrigerated or frozen piecrust dough, brought to room temperature as instructed on the package

When I have a little leftover jicama or sweet potato from making rice paper rolls (see page 63), chicken curry (see page 101), or salad (see page 163), I make these empanadas. The original rendition was deep-fried, but nowadays I often bake the filled pastries for less hassle. The filling of pork, shrimp, and jicama is classic, but I've also devised a wonderful vegetarian version (see the Notes).

This southern Viet treat is best eaten the day it's baked (refrigeration softens and dulls the shell). Consider baking some and freezing the rest for later. Refrigerated Pillsbury premade piecrusts (check near the tubes of crescent rolls at supermarkets) and Wholly Wholesome pie dough (look in the freezer case at natural food grocers) are convenient and easy to manipulate to success.

/

In a medium skillet over medium heat, warm the canola oil. Add the shallot and garlic and cook, stirring constantly, for 2 to 3 minutes, until the shallot is translucent and sweet smelling and the garlic is turning blond. Add the pork and use a wooden spoon or spatula to stir, mash, and break up the meat into small pieces. Cook for 1 to 2 minutes, until the pork is no longer pink and almost cooked through. Add the shrimp, jicama, sugar, salt, and pepper and cook, stirring frequently, for 3 to 4 minutes, until the jicama is tender.

Turn off the heat and stir in the green onion to wilt it slightly. Transfer to a small bowl, cover partially so the filling doesn't dry out, and set aside to cool. You should have about 1¼ cups. (At this point, you can transfer the filling to an airtight container and refrigerate for up to 2 days. Bring to room temperature before using.)

Preheat the oven to 400°F. Line two baking sheets with parchment paper. In a small bowl, lightly beat together the egg and water to make an egg wash; set aside.

Unroll one of the piecrusts. Using a rolling pin, roll out the crust to an 11- to 12-inch-diameter round, about ⅛ inch thick. Using a round 4-inch cookie cutter or a clean can (an empty 28-ounce tomato

/ CONTINUED

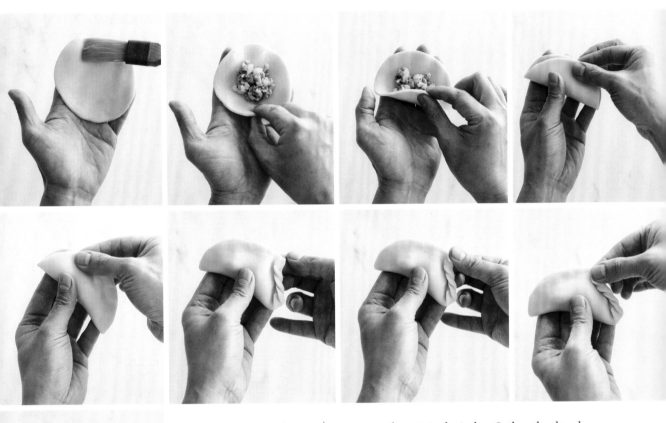

can works great), stamp out three 4-inch circles. Gather the dough scraps, gently knead into a rough ball, reroll, and stamp out another three circles. Repeat once more to eke out a total of eight circles; if the dough shrinks back as you roll, let it relax for 5 minutes and try again (commercial dough won't get tough from handling, so don't worry).

Brush some of the egg wash around the rim of each pastry round. Holding a round in one hand, use a spoon to position a brimming 1 tablespoon of filling slightly off center on the pastry round. Bring up one side to meet the other and press the edges to seal well and make a ½-inch-wide brim. For extra security, press with the tines of a fork, or get fancy and make a rope edge (see photos, above).

Place the pastries on a prepared baking sheet. Repeat with the remaining dough rounds. Then tackle the second piecrust to make another eight empanadas. (If you end up with fewer, snack on the extra filling or add it to the fried rice on page 185.)

Use a fork to poke two or three sets of holes into each empanada for ventilation, then brush the tops with egg wash. Bake for 16 to 20 minutes, until golden and tinged with brown. Let cool for about 10 minutes, and serve.

NOTES /

To freeze unbaked empanadas, place the baking sheets in the freezer for 2 hours, then transfer the empanadas to an airtight container and return to the freezer; they will keep for up to 1 month. When ready to use, partially thaw for about 25 minutes, preheat the oven, brush the empanadas with egg wash, and bake as directed.

For a **vegetarian empanada** filling, sauté the shallot and garlic over medium heat, as directed, and add 2 cups chopped fresh mushroom (white or shiitake, include stems). Cook for about 4 minutes, until the mixture has shrunk to about a third of its original volume. Add ½ cup finely diced carrot, ½ cup finely diced jicama (or sweet potato), 2 teaspoons soy sauce, ¼ teaspoon fine sea salt, and ⅛ teaspoon recently ground black pepper. Cook for 3 to 4 minutes, until the carrot and jicama are crisp-tender. If the filling seems too wet, cook a little longer. When you're satisfied, add the green onion and let the filling cool before using.

BAKED SHRIMP AND *celery toasts*

MAKES 16 TOASTS,
TO SERVE 4 TO 6

TAKES 45 MINUTES

16 rounds of French
   baguette, each about
   ⅓ inch thick; or 4 slices
   white sandwich bread,
   crusts left intact,
   quartered on the diagonal
   into triangles

12 ounces medium shrimp,
   peeled and deveined

Fine sea salt

1 large garlic clove

⅛ teaspoon recently ground
   black or white pepper

½ teaspoon sugar

1 teaspoon cornstarch

1 egg, separated

2 tablespoons canola or
   other neutral oil

⅓ cup finely chopped celery

3 tablespoons finely chopped
   green onion, white and
   green parts

1 tablespoon finely chopped
   fresh dill fronds (optional)

2½ tablespoons butter

Paprika for sprinkling

The original version of this deliciously fun snack is deep-fried. Unfortunately, it can be a grease bomb, so I prefer to bake mine for a lighter and equally delightful nibble. Shrimp toasts are terrific when prepared with sliced white sandwich bread (aka, a Pullman loaf), or rounds cut from a supermarket baguette about 2½ inches in diameter. Bread with a soft interior and crust that's not too sturdy yields delicate, crispy results. Any leftover bread can be used for a banh mi (see page 62) or Banana-Coconut Bread-Pudding Cake (page 215). Salting the shrimp returns a bit of the sea to them.

/

Preheat the oven to 300°F. Set a rack on a baking sheet. Line a second baking sheet with parchment paper.

Spread out the bread on the prepared rack and then bake for 8 to 10 minutes, until mostly dry. A little browning is okay. (Or, dry out the bread on the rack of a preheated toaster oven for 6 to 8 minutes.) Set aside to cool and crisp completely.

Increase the oven temperature to 350°F.

Toss the shrimp with about ¼ teaspoon salt, rinse immediately under lots of cold water, drain, and pat dry with paper towels. Cut the shrimp into thumbnail-size nuggets. Set aside.

To a running food processor with the feed-tube pusher removed, add the garlic and finely chop. Use a spatula to scrape down the sides. (If the chop isn't fine enough, finish with a knife or garlic press and return to the processor.) Add ½ teaspoon salt, the pepper, sugar, cornstarch, egg white, and 1½ tablespoons of the canola oil. Pulse five to eight times to blend, scraping down the sides if needed. Add the shrimp and process to a relatively coarse paste (look for a mostly smooth texture with tiny bumps). Transfer to a medium bowl, then stir in the celery, green onion, and dill (if using).

In a small saucepan over medium heat, melt the butter with the remaining 1½ teaspoons canola oil. Generously brush the mixture on one side of each toast to coat well (if one side browned more than the other, brush the lighter side); to mimic frying, do your best to use all the butter and oil. As you work, set the toasts, buttered-side down, on the parchment-lined baking sheet. With a sandwich spreader or dinner knife, spread a ¼-inch-thick layer of shrimp paste atop the unbuttered side of each toast, covering all edges and corners. (If you have leftover toasts, they're the cook's bonus.)

Break up the egg yolk with a pastry brush. Brush the tops of the toasts with the egg and sprinkle on a touch of paprika for cheery color.

Bake the toasts for about 10 minutes, until the shrimp paste has turned opaque and the toast bottoms are golden brown. Then, position a rack 4 or 5 inches from the broiler and broil the tops for 1 to 2 minutes, until slightly puffed. Let cool for 5 minutes, and serve.

NOTES /

If the shrimp is still frozen when you start out, thaw 14 to 15 ounces to ensure you have enough for the recipe.

Slightly softened, day-old baguette is easier to slice thinly. Cut it into hand-span lengths the day before and store in a zipper-top plastic bag overnight.

The bread can be dried out up to 5 days ahead and kept in an airtight container at room temperature. The shrimp paste can be made up to 2 days ahead and stored, covered, in the refrigerator.

To freeze the assembled, unbaked toasts, place on a parchment paper–lined baking sheet and put in the freezer until the toasts are solid, about 1 hour. Transfer to an airtight container, separating the layers with parchment paper. The toasts will keep in the freezer for up to 1 month. Thaw at room temperature on a parchment paper–lined baking sheet for about 1 hour. Brush with an egg wash if possible, or just sprinkle with the paprika, and bake.

banh mi sandwich

You can feature practically anything in a banh mi and it'll taste fabulous. Just remember its framework of crisp bread, a succulent filling, pickled vegetables, chile slices, cucumber, and fresh herbs. The best bread for banh mi feels light, has a thin crust, possesses a cottony interior, tastes faintly sweet, and is often considered commonplace. Be generous with the fat to avoid dry results. And don't overstuff with protein. A balanced banh mi resembles a salad in a sandwich: The visual ratio of main filling to vegetables should be 1:1 or 1:2. Create your own via this outline, which makes one sandwich.

Prep the bread. If the bread is soft, rub the crust with wet hands to moisten and then crisp in a 350°F oven (or toaster oven) for about 7 minutes. Otherwise, bake it at 325°F for 3 to 6 minutes. Let it cool a few minutes, then use a serrated bread knife to slit the bread open horizontally, maintaining a hinge, if possible. Hollow out some of the inside to make room for the filling.

Fill it up. Spread your chosen fat on the two cut sides of bread, covering all the way to the edges. (If using avocado, lay down thin slices and mash them so they adhere to the bread.) Season as you like, layer the filling on the bottom half of the bread, and top with the vegetable add-ins. Close and cut crosswise or keep whole to eat.

BREAD (CHOOSE ONE)

Small French baguette or bolillo roll

Hand-span section of French baguette

Any light, airy bread

FAT (CHOOSE ONE)

Mayonnaise (regular or flavored)

Salted European-style butter

Thin avocado slices

SEASONING (CHOOSE ONE OR MORE)

Bragg Liquid Aminos

Maggi Seasoning sauce

Soy sauce

Fine sea salt

Freshly ground black pepper

FILLING (CHOOSE ONE OR TWO)

⅓ to ½ cup thinly sliced Char Siu Chicken (page 97), Grilled Slashed Chicken (page 155), Sriracha Tofu (page 150), or Grilled Lemongrass Pork Chops (page 131)

2 fried eggs

2-egg omelet

Liver pâté or liverwurst

VEGETABLE ADD-INS
(CHOOSE ALL, SOME, OR NONE)

¼ cup Any Day Viet Pickle (page 29), drained

3 or 4 thin slices medium-hot chile, such as jalapeño or Fresno (with seeds intact for fire and fun)

4 to 6 cucumber strips, rounds, or ovals, a scant ¼ inch thick

1 to 2 tablespoons coarsely chopped or hand-torn cilantro sprigs, mint leaves, or basil leaves

JICAMA AND SAUSAGE rice paper rolls

**MAKES 12 ROLLS,
TO SERVE 4 TO 6**

TAKES ABOUT 1 HOUR

2½ teaspoons soy sauce

Brimming 2 tablespoons
  tahini

2 to 2½ tablespoons sriracha
  (use the maximum for a
  strong spicy edge)

⅓ cup hoisin sauce

1 to 1½ tablespoons water

2 eggs

Fine sea salt

3 tablespoons neutral oil

1½ tablespoons finely
  chopped garlic

One 1-pound jicama, peeled
  and cut into medium
  matchsticks

1 large handful medium
  matchstick-cut carrot
  (optional, for great color)

8 ounces fully cooked
  savory-sweet sausage
  links, cut on the diagonal
  into slices about 2 inches
  long and a scant ¼ inch
  thick (24 slices)

1 tablespoon maple syrup

¼ teaspoon Chinese
  five-spice powder

2½ cups gently packed
  baby lettuce or sliced soft
  leaf lettuce (such as butter,
  Boston, or red leaf)

12 rice papers, each
  8 inches wide

Loaded with a variety of textures and savory-sweet flavors, this Saigon street-food favorite is a close cousin of Malaysian and Singaporean *popiah* (think a colorful *mu shu* wrap). But instead of encasing the filling in a delicate wheat flour–based wrapper, Vietnamese cooks use rice paper for their rolls, which are called *bò bía*. (If rice paper seems challenging, see Rice Paper Rolls 101 on page 42 for pointers.)

The original version features sliced sweet Chinese sausages, which are unavailable at American supermarkets, so I doctor up sausages such as Aidells' mango, which are mildly sweet with tropical overtones; plus, they're fully cooked and easy to thinly slice. Garlicky stir-fried jicama, fluffy egg strips, and lettuce add complexity. The sauce is enjoyed both in the roll and on the side for dipping, resulting in a great one-two punch of flavor.

/

In a small bowl, whisk together the soy sauce, tahini, sriracha, and hoisin sauce. Taste and add enough of the water to create a salty-sweet-hot balance. Set the sauce aside. In another small bowl, beat the eggs with ⅛ teaspoon salt.

Set a small nonstick skillet over medium heat and swirl in 2 teaspoons of the oil. When hot, pour in the eggs and use a spatula to pull and push the edges toward the middle, allowing excess egg to flow out and set on the skillet. When mostly set, about 1 minute, turn the egg over. Cook for 15 to 20 seconds longer, until fully set and done, then transfer to a plate. When cooled enough to handle, cut the egg into quarters and then cut each quarter into ½-inch-wide strips. Set aside.

In a large skillet over medium heat, combine 2 tablespoons oil and the garlic. Let sizzle for 2 minutes, until light blond, then transfer to a large bowl. Turn the heat to high, add the jicama and carrot (if using) to the skillet, sprinkle in ½ teaspoon salt, and cook for 3 to 4 minutes, stirring, until crisp-tender. Add to the fried garlic and stir to combine. Set aside to cool.

/ CONTINUED

Reheat the skillet over medium-high and add the remaining 1 teaspoon oil and the sausage. Add the maple syrup and cook, stirring occasionally, for 2 to 3 minutes to caramelize the sugar and brown the sausage a bit. Remove from the heat, sprinkle in the five-spice powder, and stir to combine. Transfer to a plate and let cool.

Set up a rice paper–rolling station with the sauce, jicama, sausage, egg, lettuce, and rice papers. Nearby, have a large deep skillet or wide shallow bowl filled with 1 to 2 inches of very warm water.

For each roll, slide a rice paper round in the warm water for a few seconds to wet both sides, then place on a cutting board or dinner plate. When the rice paper is pliable, about 1 minute, smear 1½ teaspoons sauce in the center of the lower third, painting an area about 4 inches by 1 inch. Layer in 3 tablespoons lettuce, 2 to 3 tablespoons jicama, 1 or 2 egg strips, and 2 slices sausage. Bring up the bottom edge to cover the filling and roll twice. Fold in the sides and finish rolling to seal. (To replicate the photo opposite, don't place the sausage atop the egg; roll the rice paper up once, then tuck in the sausage before finishing.) Present the rolls, whole or halved, with the remaining sauce for spooning into the rolls.

NOTES /

To peel jicama, use a knife to slice off a bit of the ends to keep the tuber steady on your cutting board as you saw off its tan, tough skin. Cut the naked jicama into matchsticks by hand, or slice it in a processor (or with a box grater) before stacking and cutting into matchsticks.

The sauce, egg, sausage, and jicama can be cooked up to 2 days ahead. Refrigerate each one separately and return to room temperature before using.

For herbaceous notes, add a handful of coarsely chopped fresh mint or basil (Thai or opal are great) to the lettuce.

To make **vegetarian rolls**, swap in Sriracha Tofu (page 150) or its char siu variation for the sausage.

3

Slurp up these soupy ideas, which start out with everyday quickies, progress to simmered specials, and finish with comforting noodles in broth. Their built-in versatility enables you to take them in many Viet-ish directions.

soups

GINGERY GREENS AND *shrimp soup*

SERVES 4

TAKES 35 MINUTES

1 tablespoon canola or other neutral oil

½ medium yellow or red onion, thinly sliced

5½ cups water

Fine sea salt

1 tablespoon fish sauce, plus more as needed

One 8-ounce bunch mustard greens, coarsely chopped, including tender stems

12 large shrimp, peeled, deveined, and cut crosswise into thumbnail-width chunks, or split horizontally into symmetrical halves

1½ teaspoons finely chopped peeled ginger

Recently ground black pepper (optional)

Part of Vietnamese everyday meals, fragrant, wholesome, and fast soups like this one are called *canh*. Surprisingly, they're typically made with water and rely on gently sautéed onion, salt, and fish sauce for foundational depth. What often defines *canh* is a ton of leafy greens, cooked in the pot to contribute their flavor and nutrients. A little protein is dropped in for savory flair. At the Viet table, *canh* is not just a first course—you can help yourself to it throughout a meal to refresh your palate. This nimble soup plays well with other dishes, but you can make a light meal of it too. Just add warm bread and butter.

/

In a 3- to 4-quart saucepan over medium heat, warm the canola oil. When the oil is barely shimmering, add the onion and cook for about 4 minutes, stirring, until soft and sweetly fragrant. Add the water, ½ teaspoon salt, and fish sauce, then turn the heat to medium-high and bring to a boil. Adjust the heat to maintain a vigorous boil for 3 to 5 minutes to develop flavor. Add the greens, stirring them for even cooking. When the greens are very soft and cooked through, about 5 minutes, add the shrimp and ginger. When the shrimp are opaque and cooked through, 1 to 2 minutes, remove from the heat and let rest for 5 to 10 minutes, uncovered. Taste and add additional salt or fish sauce, if needed.

Serve the soup in a communal bowl or ladle into individual serving bowls. Sprinkle with pepper for a final spicy burst, if you like.

NOTES /

Instead of mustard greens, use another bold-flavored leaf, such as turnip greens or the radish tops left over from making pickles (see page 29). Opt for spinach for a milder taste, or combine complementary greens, like kale and mustard.

As pictured, corkscrew-shaped shrimp result from halving them horizontally. Not fond of shrimp, or maybe it's too expensive? Use a 6-ounce fish fillet, such as tilapia or rockfish. Cut the fillet into bite-size pieces to add to the soup.

embellishments

Lean, light-tasting *cháo* responds well to fatty, salty, spicy, herbal enhancements. In addition to (or instead of) garnishing your porridge with green onion and pepper, consider the following, and feel free to mix and match.

Toppings

- Crisp chopped bacon, a fried or soft-boiled egg, and maybe chopped kimchi for punch.

- Lemongrass Tempeh Crumbles (page 155) or Crispy Caramelized Pork Crumbles (page 132).

- Chopped Sriracha Tofu (page 150), fried onions or shallots, and coarsely chopped fresh cilantro, mint, or basil.

Add-ins

- Crack a raw egg into the bowl before ladling in the hot soup. Top with crumbled rice crackers and perhaps ribbons of Korean toasted seaweed snacks (one pack of *gim* is enough for a batch). Stir well before eating.

- Drop 8 ounces of raw peeled shrimp into the soup as it heats. When the shrimp are pink and cooked through, ladle out the soup. Add slivered ginger and maybe some *gim*.

- Stir in raw or seared mushroom. Add a handful of shredded cooked chicken or some shrimp, or both.

NOTES /

The soup will keep, covered, in the fridge for up to 3 days and in the freezer for up to 1 month. Splash in water when reheating to loosen it up.

For a **brown rice porridge**, replace the cooked white rice with cooked brown rice and pulse it in a food processor or blender with the 2 cups water to break up the grains. Don't add more water during the overnight soak. Cook as directed.

To make a **mixed grain porridge**, swap in ⅔ cup raw quinoa or hulled millet for 1 cup of the cooked white or brown rice; soak the grains together overnight, and proceed as directed.

TANGY SEAFOOD stew

1 tablespoon canola or other neutral oil

2 garlic cloves, finely chopped

6 cups water

1 teaspoon packed light or dark brown sugar, plus more as needed

1 tablespoon pomegranate molasses (see page 34), plus more as needed

About 1½ tablespoons fish sauce, plus more as needed

½ teaspoon fine sea salt

8 ounces fresh or frozen pineapple chunks, cut into bite-size chunks

10 ounces mild-tasting, firm fish fillet (such as snapper, tilapia, or catfish), cut into 1½-inch chunks

8 extra-large or 12 large shrimp, with or without shells, deveined

8 ounces small clams (such as Manila or littlenecks) or cockles (optional)

1 large or 2 small celery stalks, cut on a sharp diagonal into ½-inch-wide pieces

1 large unripe tomato, cut into wedges

2 cups bean sprouts

Refreshing and loaded with seafood, vegetables, and herbs, *canh chua* is a classic that evokes the bounty and easygoing rhythm of the Mekong Delta region. I used to think of it as a soup but after sharing a hearty pot with fishermen, I realized that it was more like a Viet-style bouillabaisse seafood stew. It's traditionally made with items such as tamarind, taro stem, and rice paddy herb (*ngò om*), which require a trip to an Asian market. But this streamlined version, prepared with supermarket ingredients, is a knockout.

Pomegranate molasses is a great stand-in for tamarind. Celery has more flavor than taro stem, and its leaves may be used in the herb mixture to finish the soup. The cumin mimics pungent, citrusy rice paddy herb. You can use just one kind of seafood, but adding three is an easy way to make the dish extra special. Leave the shells on the shrimp for more flavor. For a one-dish meal, serve with warm corn or flour tortillas, or fried rice.

/

In a 3- to 4-quart saucepan over medium-low heat, combine the canola oil and garlic and cook at a gentle sizzle, stirring occasionally, for about 3 minutes, until the garlic is golden. Pour in the water to arrest the cooking, then add the brown sugar, pomegranate molasses, fish sauce, salt, and pineapple. Turn the heat to high to bring to a fast simmer, adjust the heat to maintain that pace, and cook for 8 to 10 minutes to develop flavor. (If not serving right away, remove from the heat and cover; return to a near boil before continuing.)

Add the fish fillet, shrimp, and clams to the pan and cook for 3 to 4 minutes, just until the fish is opaque, the shrimp curls, and the clams open. Add the celery and cook for about 2 minutes, until slightly softened. Add the tomato and bean sprouts and cook for 1 minute more, until slightly softened, then turn off the heat. Add the herbs, cumin, and chile to the pan and then let sit for 5 minutes. Taste and, if needed, adjust the flavor with additional brown sugar, fish sauce, or pomegranate molasses to arrive at a tart-sweet-savory balance.

/ CONTINUED

⅓ cup lightly packed roughly chopped fresh herbs, such as cilantro, Thai basil, and mint, as well as celery leaves

Rounded ¼ teaspoon ground cumin

1 Fresno, jalapeño, or cayenne chile, thinly sliced

Using a two-handed approach with a ladle in one hand and chopsticks or tongs in the other, transfer the soup to a large bowl or divide among individual soup bowls. Serve immediately.

NOTES /

Most grocers sell farm-raised clams, which typically do not need to be purged of sand. Select small ones that you'd steam or use for linguine, such as sweet, tender Manilas smaller than 1½ inches wide. When using bigger clams, add them to the pot before the fish. Wait for one or two to open and then add the fish and shrimp.

Instead of pomegranate molasses, you may use tamarind liquid, concentrate, or paste. See page 35 for details and substitution ratios.

Instead of celery, use 12 medium okra, cut crosswise into 1-inch pieces; or 1 small zucchini, quartered and cut crosswise into 1-inch pieces.

VELVETY CORN AND coconut soup

SERVES 4

TAKES 45 MINUTES

3 large ears fresh sweet corn

Rounded 1 tablespoon virgin coconut oil

½ medium yellow onion, chopped

3 cups water

Fine sea salt

5 dried shiitake mushrooms, soaked in hot water for 15 minutes and then drained

Chile oil for drizzling

About 1 tablespoon chopped fresh cilantro

One summer, I gave my neighbor, Dan, some Thai chiles for a recipe; in return, he piled six ears of homegrown yellow corn by my backdoor. It was late in the season, and he said he'd harvested "what the horses hadn't eaten." The mature kernels were super-sweet, reminiscent of the canned creamed corn that my mom used to make into a creamy corn and shiitake soup. This got me thinking about how corn, coconut, and chile make such good friends (sweet, fatty, and hot!). That is how I ended up with this simple, elegant soup. Chile oil, such as Lee Kum Kee brand, works fine.

/

Shuck the corn, then cut the kernels off the cob to yield about 3 cups. Use your hands to break the cobs in half and then set aside.

In a 3- to 4-quart saucepan over medium heat, melt the coconut oil. Add the onion and cook, stirring occasionally, for about 4 minutes, until fragrant and soft. Add the corn kernels and cobs, water, and ¾ teaspoon salt and bring to a boil, then adjust the heat to cook at a simmer, uncovered, for 20 minutes. The corn will be tender, yet crunchy.

Meanwhile, gently squeeze the shiitakes to expel excess moisture, then trim the stems and thinly slice or quarter the caps and set aside.

Remove the pan from the heat and let the soup rest, uncovered, for 10 minutes to cool and intensify. Remove and discard the cobs. Transfer the soup to a blender and puree until super-smooth. Strain the puree through a mesh strainer positioned over a pot, stirring and pressing on the solids.

Add the mushrooms to the pot and rewarm the soup over medium heat, stirring frequently to prevent scorching, for 5 to 10 minutes, until the mushrooms are plump and the flavors have melded. If necessary, add water to thin the soup or simmer to thicken it.

Divide the soup among four bowls. For a savory hit, garnish with a tiny pinch of salt, add a small drizzle of chile oil, and sprinkle with the cilantro. Serve immediately.

WONTONS IN gingery broth

SERVES 4 TO 6

TAKES ABOUT 1½ HOURS

2 green onions

5 ounces ground pork or chicken thigh, or finely chopped raw shrimp

½ teaspoon cornstarch, plus more for dusting

Fine sea salt

1 pinch recently ground black or white pepper

⅛ teaspoon sugar, plus more as needed

½ teaspoon toasted sesame oil or chile oil, plus more for garnish

Rounded ¼ teaspoon grated peeled ginger (optional, use for a zippy filling), plus 3 quarter-size slices unpeeled ginger, bruised

30 square wonton wrappers

4½ cups chicken stock (see page 36), vegetable stock (see page 38), or store-bought chicken or vegetable broth

⅔ cup sliced vegetables, such as carrot, snow peas, or mushroom, or a combination

I've been making and eating wontons since I was a kid, and I loved them then as much as I do now. When served in broth they're called *súp hoành thánh* and are slippery, cozy, and filled with a savory surprise. The beauty of wontons (and dumplings, in general) is that they can contain different things. If you want meat, go with the main recipe. If not, try the terrific tofu filling in the Notes.

You can buy wonton wrappers, which are square and roughly 3-inches wide, at many supermarkets; Dynasty and Nasoya are well-distributed brands. If they're unavailable, use round gyoza wrappers or cut 6-inch eggroll skins into quarters. Parboiling the wontons prevents the wrappers' starch from clouding up the broth. Choose sesame oil for a classic flavor; chile oil injects rich heat. If you like, use one type of oil for the filling and the other for a garnish. Omit the vegetables to focus solely on the wontons. This recipe is long, but many steps can be done in advance.

/

Mince all the white part and some of the green part of 1 green onion to get 1 tablespoon and transfer to a medium bowl. Thinly slice the remaining green part and reserve for a garnish. Cut the second green onion into 3-inch lengths and bruise them with the flat side of a knife blade; set aside.

Add the pork, cornstarch, ¼ teaspoon salt, pepper, sugar, sesame oil, and grated ginger (if using) to the minced green onion in the bowl. Vigorously stir with a fork to blend well, then cover with plastic wrap and set aside for about 15 minutes to develop flavor. (At this point, the filling can be stored, in the fridge, for up to 1 day.)

When you're ready to assemble the wontons, line a baking sheet with parchment paper and dust well with cornstarch.

Lay 4 to 6 wrappers on your work surface and paint the edges with water. Using two small spoons, scoop 1 teaspoon of the filling and place slightly off center on each wrapper. Bring up a corner of the

/ CONTINUED

wrapper to meet the opposite corner to create a triangle, or bring up one side to meet the opposite side to get a rectangle. Use your thumb and index finger to seal the edges well and press out any air bubbles. Or, keep going and fancy up the wontons by bringing together two opposite corners, overlapping them slightly, then pressing to seal (add a dot of water for security). You'll create shapes like the ones pictured here. Place the wontons on the prepared baking sheet so they are not touching. Repeat with the remaining filling and wonton wrappers. Loosely cover with plastic wrap; keep at room temperature if using soon, or refrigerate up to 3 hours.

Fill a large pot halfway with water and bring to a boil over high heat, covering and lowering the heat to keep hot, as needed.

Meanwhile, in a 3- to 4-quart saucepan over high heat, bring the chicken stock, sliced ginger, and bruised green onion to a boil. Lower the heat to gently simmer for 10 to 15 minutes to develop a little gingery flavor. When satisfied, discard the solids and add the sliced vegetables, partially cover, and adjust the heat to a gentle simmer.

Return the large pot of water to a boil and add all the wontons, gently dropping them in one at a time and using a wooden spoon to nudge them to prevent sticking. When the water returns to a gentle boil, adjust the heat to maintain that cooking pace. After the wontons have floated to the top, let them cook for another 2 minutes, until translucent. Scoop them up with a spider skimmer or slotted spoon, pausing above the pot to allow excess water to drip down. Slide the wontons into the hot broth, increase the heat under the broth slightly, and let the wontons soak up some of the broth and finish cooking, about 1 minute.

Divide the wontons and vegetables among individual soup bowls or transfer to a large serving bowl. Taste the broth and add pinches of salt or sugar, if necessary, to create a savory-sweet finish. Ladle the broth over the wontons and add a dash of sesame oil. Top with the thinly sliced green onion and serve immediately.

NOTES /

If using shrimp, finely chop with a knife; or cut each one into blueberry-size nuggets. Put a handful into a small food processor and pulse four to six times. Transfer the sticky mass to a bowl and repeat with the remaining shrimp.

Once filled and shaped, the uncooked wontons may be frozen on the baking sheet until hard, about 1 hour, then transferred to an airtight container and returned to the freezer for up to 1 month. Partially thaw before boiling.

For a **tofu wonton filling**, use about 6 ounces extra-firm tofu. Break up the block into three or four chunks and put them into a piece of muslin or clean non-terry kitchen towel. Standing over a sink, squeeze and massage to expel liquid and mash the tofu into bits. When little water comes out, transfer to a bowl. Mix in the cornstarch, ⅛ teaspoon salt, the pepper, sugar, and 1 tablespoon minced green onion. Add the sesame oil and 2 teaspoons soy sauce and stir vigorously to combine and compact into a dense mixture. Finish as directed.

CHICKEN AND glass noodle soup

**SERVES 4 AS A LIGHT LUNCH
OR 6 TO 8 AS A STARTER**

TAKES ABOUT 45 MINUTES

Chubby ¾-inch (¾-ounce)
  section ginger, peeled,
  sliced into 3 or 4 coins,
  and bruised

2 medium-large green onions,
  white parts kept whole and
  bruised, green parts sliced
  into thin rings

6 cups chicken stock (see
  page 36) or store-bought
  chicken broth

2 cups water

Fine sea salt

6 ounces boneless, skinless
  chicken breast

2 medium-large dried
  shiitake mushrooms

5 ounces dried glass noodles
  (saifun or bean thread
  noodles; see page 14)

1½ tablespoons fish sauce,
  plus more as needed

2 teaspoons maple syrup, or
  1 teaspoon sugar (optional)

2 rounded tablespoons finely
  chopped fresh cilantro

Recently ground black pepper

2 tablespoons fried onions or
  shallots (optional)

1 large Thai or medium
  serrano chile, thinly sliced,
  with seeds intact (optional)

1 lime, cut into wedges
  (optional)

This classic Viet noodle soup, called *miến gà*, is easy to prepare.
Some versions are made with giblets for textural fun, but I stick to
a simpler preparation that involves doctoring up homemade stock
or store-bought broth. For depth of flavor and greater efficiency,
I cook the chicken and rehydrate the mushroom in the simmering
broth. Lots of herbs and fried shallot or onion (the kind you'd use
in a green bean casserole at Thanksgiving) finish the bowl with
flair. If Vietnamese coriander (*rau răm*, aka hot mint) is available,
swap it for the cilantro for a wonderful herbal bite. For a nice lunch,
pair this soup with a salad from chapter 7.

/

Warm a 3- to 4-quart saucepan over medium heat. Add the ginger and
bruised white parts of the green onions and cook, stirring, for 30 seconds, until aromatic. Remove from the heat, wait about 15 seconds to
cool briefly, then add the chicken stock, water, and ½ teaspoon salt.
Bring to a boil over high heat, then drop in the chicken breast and
mushrooms. When the liquid starts bubbling at the edges, remove from
the heat, cover tightly, and let stand for 20 minutes to gently poach.
The chicken breast should be firm, yet still yield a bit to the touch
(press on it to test). Remove and discard the ginger and green onion.

Transfer the chicken to a bowl, flush with cold running water to
arrest the cooking, and then drain. When cool enough to handle,
about 10 minutes, shred with your fingers into bite-size pieces,
pulling the meat along its natural grain, and return to the bowl.
Retrieve the mushrooms from the broth, stem, thinly slice, and add
to the chicken. Cover loosely to prevent drying out. (At this point,
you may transfer the chicken and mushrooms and the broth to
separate airtight containers and store, in the fridge, for up to 2 days.
Bring to room temperature before using.)

Meanwhile, soak the noodles in hot water to cover for 5 to 10 minutes,
or until pliable. Drain, and snip with kitchen scissors into 6-inch
lengths. Set aside.

Rewarm the broth over medium-high heat and, as it heats up, add the fish sauce and season with the maple syrup and salt, if needed, to create a savory-sweet finish. Add the chicken, mushrooms, and noodles; as soon the soup returns to a boil, remove from the heat. The noodles will have become clear and plump. Taste again to recheck the seasonings, adding a glug of fish sauce or pinches of salt, as needed.

Ladle the soup into individual bowls (use chopsticks or tongs to move slippery noodles into the ladle) and garnish with the green onion rings, cilantro, a generous sprinkling of pepper, and the fried onions, if desired. Serve immediately, passing the chile slices and lime wedges at the table.

SUPERMARKET STOCK OPTIONS: BROTH BUYING GUIDE

Bewildered by the variety of commercially made broths sold at American supermarkets, I once bought a dozen brands and did a tasting. There were differences on many levels, including flavor (chicken noodle-ish brews versus chicken-y essence), thickness (from light and clear to thick and murky), and the amount of sodium ("low sodium" can range from 140 mg to 570 mg per 1 cup).

For the purposes of matching homemade, select brands with shorter ingredients lists; they're easier to manipulate for recipes in this book. At the time of this writing, my favorite brands of chicken and beef broth include Swanson low-sodium and 365 Everyday Value regular (the Whole Foods brand). Also good is O Organics (the Albertsons supermarket brand) vegetable broth, which is golden hued and relatively clear. I use those brands' ingredients lists and sodium levels as benchmarks for comparison shopping. That's how I can gauge if there's a new brand to try.

SMOKED TURKEY pho

SERVES 4

TAKES ABOUT 1¼ HOURS

BROTH

One 1⅓-pound smoked turkey thigh

One 4-ounce Fuji apple, peeled, cored, and cut into thumbnail-size chunks

One 2-ounce celery stalk, coarsely chopped

One 3-ounce carrot, sliced (scrub and use unpeeled, if you like)

8 ounces napa or regular green cabbage leaves, cut into large pieces

One 1-ounce bunch fresh cilantro, stems and leaves, coarsely chopped

3 star anise (24 robust points total)

2 whole cloves

2 teaspoons coriander seeds

1 slender 3-inch cinnamon stick

Chubby 2-inch (2-ounce) section ginger, peeled, thinly sliced, and bruised

One 10-ounce yellow onion, halved and thickly sliced

Fine sea salt

About 1½ tablespoons fish sauce

About 2 teaspoons maple syrup, or 1 teaspoon sugar (optional)

Vietnam's national dish, pho noodle soup, is surprisingly flexible and democratic. There are many great renditions, in addition to the classic beef and chicken. This version is terrific because it's not just for Thanksgiving, it's deliciously convenient—smoked turkey parts are sold year-round at many grocery stores. They are fully cooked, with big flavor, so there's less of a time commitment and hassle involved in making a batch of fabulous pho. A pressure cooker speeds things along, but there's a stockpot option in the Notes. Weigh the ingredients to dial in flavors.

/

To make the broth Give the smoked turkey a very quick spray or rinse of water to remove visible impurities. Set in a large bowl and add the apple, celery, carrot, cabbage, and cilantro. Keep near the stove.

In a 6-quart pressure cooker, combine the star anise, cloves, coriander seeds, and cinnamon stick and place over medium heat. Toast the spices for 3 to 4 minutes, shaking or stirring, until fragrant, then add the ginger and yellow onion and sear, stirring, for 45 to 60 seconds, until fragrant; a little browning is okay. (If using a multicooker, use a medium heat setting, such as Sauté on the Fagor Lux, or adjust the Sauté function to "normal" on the Instant Pot.)

Add 4 cups water to the cooker to arrest the cooking process. (If using a multicooker, add 3½ cups water.) Add the turkey, apple, vegetables, 1½ teaspoons salt, and another 4 cups water. If the ingredients, including the water, fill more than two-thirds of the pot (its maximum fill line), remove some of the water. You can add more later, after cooking and straining.

Lock the lid in place. Bring to high pressure, adjust the heat to maintain pressure, and cook for 15 minutes. Then, remove from the heat, depressurize naturally for 25 minutes, and release the residual pressure. (If using a multicooker, program it to cook at high pressure for 15 minutes, turn it off or unplug it, and depressurize for 30 minutes before releasing residual pressure.)

Unlock the lid and, once the bubbling stops, retrieve the turkey, rinsing with water to cool and prevent it from drying out. When

BOWLS

10 ounces dried narrow flat rice noodles (pad thai noodles), boiled in unsalted water until chewy-tender (cooking times vary with brand), rinsed under cool water, and drained

½ small yellow or red onion, very thinly sliced against the grain, soaked in water for 10 minutes, and drained

2 green onions, green parts only, thinly sliced

¼ cup chopped fresh cilantro, leafy tops only

Recently ground black pepper

OPTIONAL ADD-INS

4 handfuls bean sprouts

1 thinly sliced chile, such as jalapeño, serrano, or Fresno

4 to 6 mint sprigs

1 lime, cut into wedges

Hoisin sauce

Sriracha

cool enough to handle, remove the meat and discard the skin, if you like. Cut the meat into pieces that are small enough to manage with chopsticks, then set aside.

Strain the broth (there should be little fat to skim) through a fine-mesh strainer positioned over a 3- or 4-quart saucepan. (Line the strainer with muslin for a super-clear broth.) When cool enough to handle, press and squeeze on the solids to expel more broth. Discard the solids. You should have 8 cups; if needed, place over high heat and boil down to concentrate flavors or add water to dilute. (The broth and turkey can be kept in separate airtight containers and refrigerated for up to 3 days or frozen for up to 3 months. Reheat before using.) Season the broth with fish sauce. If it still needs a bold, savory-sweet finish, add more salt and the maple syrup.

To assemble the bowls While the broth cooks, or about 30 minutes before serving, cook the noodles. Divide among four noodle-soup bowls and top with the turkey, arranging the pieces in one flat layer to ensure they get warmed by the broth. If the noodles and turkey are cold, warm them in a microwave with 30-second blasts. Crown each bowl with yellow onion, green onion, cilantro, and black pepper.

Bring the broth to a simmer over medium heat. Recheck its flavor to make sure it tastes strong. Raise the heat, bring it to a boil, and then ladle about 2 cups of broth into each bowl. Serve with the bean sprouts, sliced chile, mint, lime wedges, hoisin, and sriracha at the table. Invite diners to add as many add-ins as they wish.

NOTE /

To make the broth in a 6- to 8-quart stockpot, toast the spices and sear the ginger and onion over medium heat. When aromatic, add 5 cups water, the turkey, apple, vegetables, cilantro, salt, and another 5 cups water. Partially cover and bring to a simmer over high heat. Uncover and skim off the scum. Adjust the heat to gently simmer for 1 hour, uncovered, until heady and savory-sweet, and proceed as directed.

ROAST CHICKEN NOODLE soup

SERVES 4

TAKES ABOUT 1 HOUR

4 large or 6 small dried
shiitake mushrooms

2 cups hot water

2 medium-large green onions

1 tablespoon toasted
sesame oil, plus more
for drizzling

Chubby 1-inch (1-ounce)
section ginger, peeled,
cut into 4 or 5 coins,
and bruised

6 cups chicken stock (see
page 36) or store-bought
chicken broth

10 ounces deboned
rotisserie chicken or roast
chicken, cut into bite-size
pieces, plus the leftover
chicken carcass, bones,
unwanted parts, pan juices,
and skin

½ teaspoon plus ⅛ teaspoon
Chinese five-spice powder

Fine sea salt

2 teaspoons maple syrup,
or 1 teaspoon sugar

1½ tablespoons soy sauce

8 ounces dried Chinese
wheat noodles, ramen, or
soba, boiled according the
package directions and
drained

¼ cup coarsely chopped
fresh cilantro

The next time you roast a chicken, such as for the honey-hoisin chicken on page 104, save the leftovers for this satisfying noodle soup, called *mì gà* in Vietnamese. Save unwanted bits—bones, pan juices—and add them to the broth for extra oomph. Cut or shred the succulent flesh for the topping. To get the required 10 ounces, debone half a breast plus a thigh or drumstick from a roast chicken, or two chicken thighs. If you're short on meat, boil a few eggs and add them, halved, to the soup bowls. (You can cook the eggs in the pot you'll use to boil your noodles.)

Wheat-based Chinese noodles (see page 14) are typically used for this soup, but it's great with ramen (regular or instant) or soba noodles. Baby bok choy has delicate, sweet flavor; the jade green Shanghai variety is very common.

/

Place the mushrooms in a medium bowl, add 1 cup of the hot water, and let soak for 15 minutes. Strain the mushrooms, reserving the soaking liquid, and set aside.

Meanwhile, thinly slice the green parts of the green onions to get 3 tablespoons and set aside for garnish. Cut the remainder into pinkie-finger lengths and bruise them.

In a 4-quart saucepan over medium heat, warm the sesame oil. Add the bruised green onion and ginger and cook until aromatic, about 1 minute. Add the chicken stock, chicken bits, mushroom soaking liquid, and remaining 1 cup water. Partially cover, bring to a boil over high heat, then adjust the heat to a simmer. Skim off any scum that rises to the surface and add the five-spice powder, 1 teaspoon salt, maple syrup, and soy sauce. Simmer, uncovered, for 30 minutes, then remove from the heat and let rest for 5 minutes. If needed, skim off any fat.

Pour the broth through a mesh strainer into a clean pot. (Line the strainer with muslin for super-clear broth.) You should have 7 cups; if needed, return to the stove top and boil down to concentrate flavors or add water to dilute.

/ CONTINUED

10 ounces baby bok choy, halved lengthwise and cut diagonally into pieces about 1 inch wide and 2 inches long

Recently ground black or white pepper, or Japanese togarashi

½ cup Any Day Viet Pickle (page 29; optional)

Stem and quarter the shiitake mushrooms, then add to the broth. (At this point, you can transfer the mushrooms and broth to an air-tight container and refrigerate for up to 2 days.) Return the broth to a simmer over high heat, adjusting the heat to maintain a simmer.

Meanwhile, divide the noodles among four noodle-soup bowls. Arrange the chicken on top in one layer. If the noodles and chicken are cold, warm them in the microwave with 20-second blasts. Top with the sliced green onion and cilantro.

Add the bok choy to the simmering broth and cook for about 1 minute, until bright green and slightly soft. Taste and, if needed, season the broth with more salt, ¼ teaspoon at a time. Raise the heat and bring to a boil, then divide the broth and vegetables among the bowls. Drizzle with sesame oil and sprinkle with pepper. Serve, and have diners add the pickle to their bowls for bright flavor and crunch.

NOTES /

If dried shiitake mushrooms are unavailable, use 6 medium fresh shiitake, white button, or cremini mushrooms. There won't be any soaking liquid, so add an additional 1 cup water to the broth.

Leave the chicken skin on for authenticity, or toss it into the brewing broth.

SPICY HUE NOODLE soup

SERVES 4

TAKES ABOUT 1½ HOURS

BROTH

1½ pounds pork spareribs,
cut across the bones into
2- to 3-inch-wide strips
(ask a butcher to do this)

16 ounces bone-in beef
shank (sold as crosscut
slices, about 1 inch thick)

Fine sea salt

Recently ground black pepper

1 tablespoon canola or other
neutral oil, plus more as
needed

1 medium-large yellow onion,
cut into 1-inch chunks

2 hefty or 3 medium stalks
lemongrass, untrimmed,
cut into 3-inch lengths and
bruised with a meat mallet
or heavy saucepan

Rounded 1 teaspoon paprika
or ground annatto

2 pounds beef leg bones
(marrow and knuckle; 2- to
3-inch pieces are best)

One 4-ounce Fuji apple,
peeled, cored, and cut into
thumbnail-size chunks

1½ tablespoons fish sauce

1 tablespoon anchovy paste

About 2 teaspoons maple
syrup, or 1 teaspoon sugar
(optional)

Want to go beyond pho? Make Vietnam's second signature noodle soup—*bún bò Huế* (BBH), popular in the city of Hue and elsewhere in the central region. It's a lusty bowl with lemongrass, chile, and fat round rice noodles. Reflecting the area's gutsy spirit, the cooked beef and pork are *just* tender, not fork-tender. The classic broth owes its alluring color to annatto (a natural colorant common in cheese and snack foods), and its slight cloudiness and umami funk to fermented shrimp sauce (*mắm tôm*). Whereas pho is elegantly subtle, BBH looks like a wild party in a bowl.

Finding supermarket ingredients for BBH was challenging until I realized that anchovy paste (shelved in the canned fish section) is a worthy stand-in for the shrimp sauce. Rice spaghetti is a perfect sub for the extra-large *bún* (round rice noodles) that are sold at Asian markets. And ordinary paprika yields cheerful color like annatto, which some markets carry in the spices section.

Extreme BBH often includes pork hocks, congealed pork blood, snappy pork sausage, and shredded banana blossom, but you don't need all that for a thrilling bowl. This elemental version comes very close to the classic with beef shank and pork ribs (a balance of lean meat, fat, and cartilage, with bones to boost the broth). A pressure cooker quickly renders big flavors; use recently boiled water to bring the cooker to pressure faster to avoid overly tender meats. If you prefer, use the stockpot method in the Notes. Many steps of this long recipe can be done in advance.

/

To make the broth Bring a kettle of water to a boil, then lower the heat to keep hot. Cut the strips of ribs between the bones into three or four shorter sections. Lightly season the ribs and beef shank with salt and pepper.

In a 6-quart pressure cooker over medium-high heat, warm the canola oil. (If using a multicooker, use a high heat setting, such as Brown on the Fagor Lux, or adjust the Sauté function on the Instant Pot.) In batches, lightly brown the meat, about 1 minute per side, and set aside.

/ CONTINUED

CHILE-LEMONGRASS MIX

2½ tablespoons canola or other neutral oil

1½ tablespoons red chili flakes

1½ teaspoons minced garlic

2 tablespoons minced lemongrass, or 1½ tablespoons grated lemongrass

½ teaspoon sugar

1¼ teaspoons fish sauce

BOWLS

12 ounces dried rice spaghetti, boiled in unsalted water until chewy-tender (cooking times vary with brand), rinsed under cool water, and drained

½ small yellow or red onion, sliced very thinly against the grain, soaked in water for 10 minutes, and drained

2 thinly sliced green onions, green part only

¼ cup chopped fresh cilantro, leafy tops only

OPTIONAL ADD-INS

2 to 3 cups thinly sliced romaine lettuce or shaved green cabbage

3 handfuls bean sprouts

1 or 2 limes, cut into wedges

4 to 6 sprigs fresh mint

Add a splash of oil to the cooker, if needed, then the onion and lemongrass and cook, stirring, until fragrant, about 1 minute. Add the paprika and stir until fragrant, 10 to 15 seconds, then add 4 cups hot water to arrest the cooking process. (If using a multicooker, add 3½ cups water.) Add the beef bones, seared ribs and beef shank, apple, 1½ teaspoons fine sea salt, fish sauce, and 4 cups hot water. If the ingredients, including the water, fill more than two-thirds of the pot (its maximum fill line), remove some of the water. You can add more later, after cooking and straining.

Lock the lid in place. Bring to high pressure, adjust the heat to maintain pressure, and cook for 16 minutes. Then, remove from the heat, depressurize naturally for 20 minutes, and release the residual pressure. (If using a multicooker, program it to cook at high pressure for 16 minutes, turn it off or unplug it, and depressurize for 25 minutes before releasing residual pressure.) Have the anchovy paste and maple syrup (if using) ready for finishing the broth.

To make the chile-lemongrass mix While the broth cooks, in a small saucepan over medium-low heat, combine the canola oil, red chili flakes, garlic, and lemongrass and bring to a gentle simmer. Lower the heat to gently bubble and sizzle for 3 minutes, until fragrant and orange; swirl or stir occasionally for even cooking. Remove from the heat and stir in the sugar and fish sauce. Transfer to a small serving bowl and let cool completely. (The mix can be transferred to an airtight container and stored, in the fridge, for up to 5 days.)

Unlock the cooker and, once the bubbling stops, use a metal ladle to remove as much fat as you like. Use tongs to transfer the ribs and shank to a bowl filled with water; if bones fall off, that's fine. Soak for 10 minutes, to avoid dry meat, then drain, partially cover, and set aside. Fish out and discard the remaining large, bulky solids from the broth.

/ CONTINUED

Strain the broth through a fine-mesh strainer positioned over a 3- or 4-quart saucepan. (Line the strainer with muslin for super-clear broth.) You should have 8 cups; if needed, place over high heat and boil down to concentrate flavors or add water to dilute. (At this point, you can let the meats and broth cool, then transfer to separate airtight containers and refrigerate for up to 3 days or freeze up to 3 months. Return to room temperature before continuing. You can defat after chilling too.)

To finish the broth and assemble the bowls In a small bowl, whisk the anchovy paste with 2 tablespoons of the broth until smooth, and add to the remaining broth. Sweeten with the maple syrup and, if needed, add more salt, ¼ teaspoon at a time, for a strong savory-sweet flavor. To establish a moderately spicy edge, add 1 to 1½ tablespoons of the chile-lemongrass mix.

About 30 minutes before serving, cook the noodles. Divide among four noodle-soup bowls. (To save time, you can prep the noodles while the broth cooks.)

Warm the broth over medium-high heat. Meanwhile, cut the ribs between the bones or through the cartilage; then debone the beef shank and cut or pull the meat into bite-size pieces. Add the pork and beef pieces to the broth. (Or, for more elegance and less stringiness, keep the beef in large pieces and slice at an angle or across the grain, then arrange on the noodles in each bowl; the broth will warm the beef.)

Bring the broth to a boil, then divide the meat and broth among the soup bowls. Top with the yellow onion, green onion, and cilantro. Serve the lettuce, bean sprouts, lime, mint, and remaining chile-lemongrass mix at the table. Have diners add whatever add-ins they wish. The produce lends texture, lime and mint brighten, and the chile-lemongrass mixture injects a unique toasty note and oomph.

NOTES /

If you like cartilage, use rib tips, the 2- to 3-inch-wide strip trimmed from a slab of spareribs to create St. Louis–style ribs. Buy a 4- to 5-pound slab of spareribs and ask the butcher to trim the tips for this soup; the remaining rack is perfect for the riblets recipe on page 125. Otherwise, get half a rack of ribs and have the butcher cut it as directed.

If beef shank is unavailable, use brisket or boneless chuck. Thinly slice the beef and place atop the noodles during bowl assembly. If you can't find spaghetti rice noodles (see page 15), boil up dried Chinese wheat noodles or regular spaghetti.

To make the broth in an 8-quart stockpot, boil the beef leg bones in water to just cover for 1 to 2 minutes. Drain in the sink, rinse, and set aside. Wash and dry the pot, then sear and sauté the ingredients as directed. Add 10 cups water along with the bones, meat, apple, and fish sauce. Bring to boil over high heat, then adjust the heat to gently simmer, uncovered, for 2 hours. Do your best to skim off the surface scum and occasionally check to make sure the meat is submerged; add water, if needed.

After 1½ hours of cooking, check to the ribs; if they are just tender, remove and soak in a bowl of water. If not, keep in the pot and continue cooking with the shank for another 30 minutes, until both are tender. As needed, add ½ cup water and simmer for another 30 minutes. When satisfied, let the meats cool, strain the broth, and continue with the recipe.

SIMPLE INGREDIENT SWAPS FOR FANTASTIC BROTH

Instead of using Chinese rock sugar, an Asian-market ingredient, to impart a round sweetness to stocks and broth, I often substitute a 4-ounce Fuji apple. It's an easy way to build the savory-sweet notes of umami. If you like, use another sweet apple variety or a mildly sweet Tokyo turnip in equal weight. When finishing a broth, maple syrup or sugar (organic cane sugar has a rounder, deeper flavor) may be used to add an extra hint of sweetness and refine flavors. It's unusual to employ these ingredients in soup, but I assure you that they make a difference.

4

Moving from chicken to shrimp and shellfish and then into fish, these recipes offer easygoing, flavorful ideas for you to build a Viet menu or to pair with non-Viet foods. There are terrific one-dish meals too.

CHICKEN AND
seafood

CHAR SIU chicken

SERVES 4

TAKES 45 MINUTES

1¾ pounds boneless, skinless chicken thighs

1 large garlic clove, put through a press or minced and mashed

¼ teaspoon Chinese five-spice powder

2 tablespoons honey, preferably amber colored

Brimming 2 tablespoons hoisin sauce

1½ tablespoons soy sauce

1 tablespoon ketchup

Scant 2 teaspoons toasted sesame oil

Savory-sweet and garlicky Chinese barbecued pork, called *char siu* in Cantonese and *xá xíu* in Vietnamese, is hard to resist. Since the classic porky version requires a good hour (better yet, overnight) to marinate, my weeknight approach is to make it with chicken thighs and grill it for a wonderful old-school flavor. You can use a stove-top grill pan as suggested here, or prepare a medium charcoal fire or preheat a gas grill to medium and cook the chicken for 10 to 12 minutes, basting during the last 3 minutes. Enjoy *char siu* chicken for dinner with rice and a quick stir-fried vegetable or a salad. Use leftovers (or make a double batch) for banh mi (see page 62), a noodle soup, or fried rice (see page 185).

/

Pat the chicken thighs with paper towels to remove excess moisture, then trim and discard any big fat pads. If the thighs are large or super-uneven in thickness, butterfly each one. Lay the thigh, smooth-side down, on your cutting board. Wielding your knife horizontally, slash the big mound of flesh to create a flap of meat, stopping just shy of cutting all the way through. Fold back the meat flap that you just created. The thigh should now be about 50 percent longer and relatively even in thickness. If the result seems awkwardly large, cut it crosswise into two smaller, square-ish pieces. Set aside.

In a large bowl, stir together the garlic, five-spice powder, honey, hoisin, soy sauce, ketchup, and sesame oil. Remove 3 tablespoons and set aside for glazing the chicken. Add the chicken to the bowl, coating the pieces well. Cover with plastic wrap and marinate at room temperature for 30 minutes, or refrigerate up to 24 hours (return to room temperature before cooking).

Lightly oil a cast-iron stove-top grill pan and set over medium-high heat. Add the chicken and cook for 6 to 10 minutes, turning several times. To test for doneness, pierce the flesh with the tip of a knife; the chicken is cooked when clear juices flow out. During the last 2 minutes, when the chicken feels firmish, baste with the reserved marinade to freshen flavor and add sheen. Transfer to a platter and let rest for 5 to 10 minutes before serving.

GRILLED SLASHED *chicken*

SERVES 4

TAKES 45 MINUTES

2 garlic cloves, roughly
  chopped

¼ cup roughly chopped
  shallot or yellow onion

1 teaspoon sugar

½ teaspoon fine sea salt

½ teaspoon recently ground
  black pepper

2 to 3 teaspoons fish sauce

1 teaspoon water (optional)

4 small whole chicken legs
  (about 2 pounds total)

When I first had this grilled chicken on Phu Quoc island (a hub for excellent fish sauce, located off the southern coast of Vietnam), a free-range chicken was chopped through the bone, marinated, and grilled as part of a feast of many dishes. About a dozen of us nibbled on the chicken with abandon as we guzzled cold beer. It was marvelous, and not because of the all the beer. Cutting up the chicken exposed more of it to the seasonings, which is what made it taste extra good. Plus, the small pieces cooked up quickly and evenly.

At home, instead of buying an entire chicken and hacking it up, I opt for chicken legs or thighs and slash them down to the bone. The marinade gets into the meat and under the skin to yield very tasty results. Grill some vegetables while you grill the chicken, and serve with rice for a terrific meal. Use leftovers for banh mi (see page 62). If small legs are unavailable, use 8 small or 3 medium bone-in thighs.

/

In a small food processor, combine the garlic, shallot, sugar, salt, pepper, and 2 teaspoons fish sauce. Whirl into a relatively smooth mixture, pausing to scrape down the sides and, if necessary, adding the water to facilitate things. Taste and add up to 1 teaspoon fish sauce to create a savory-sweet-pungent finish. (Or, use a mortar and pestle to render the solid ingredients into a paste and then stir in the fish sauce.) Transfer the marinade to a large bowl.

Pat the chicken legs with paper towels to remove excess moisture, then trim any excess skin flaps. Position each leg flatter-side down on your cutting board. Cut two slashes across each thigh and two slashes across each drumstick in their thicker parts, cutting down to the bone. Flip the legs and slash twice on the thigh and once on the drumstick.

Add the chicken to the marinade, rubbing the marinade into the crevices and under the skin. Cover with plastic wrap and marinate at room temperature for 20 minutes, or refrigerate overnight (return to room temperature before grilling).

Prepare a medium charcoal fire or preheat a gas grill to medium (you can hold your hand 6 inches above the grill for 4 to 5 seconds). Grill the chicken for 16 to 20 minutes, turning frequently, until cooked through (poke or cut into the thickest part, and the juices flowing out should be clear). Transfer to a platter and let rest for 5 to 10 minutes before serving.

GET MORE CLUCK FOR YOUR BUCK

When I started cooking for myself, I made a lot of food from cheap chickens. They were what I could afford. My food was good, but when I splurged on higher-quality birds, my food was fabulous. Every now and then, I test my recipes with cheap chickens, but I always learn the same lesson: It's never the deal that it seems to be. The flavor and texture is flabby and there's often a fair amount of liquid in the packaging to make the net weight of the chicken not much of a savings. Plus, you don't get to pick the pieces you want.

If possible, shop for chicken at a butcher counter where you can select what you need. And, if you can afford it, select air-chilled chicken—its flesh is firmer with greater savory depth, and the skin cooks up crisp and delicate. You may spend a little more but you'll likely feel satisfied by eating less of it too.

COCONUT-KISSED chicken and chile

SERVES 4

TAKES 20 MINUTES

4 medium-large boneless, skinless chicken thighs (about 1⅔ pounds total)

1 teaspoon grated or minced and mashed peeled ginger

1½ teaspoons cornstarch

Rounded ¼ teaspoon fine sea salt

1½ teaspoons Caramel Sauce (page 32), or 1 teaspoon molasses

1 tablespoon fish sauce

¾ cup coconut water, plus more as needed

¼ to ½ teaspoon sugar (optional)

1½ tablespoons virgin coconut oil

1½ tablespoons finely chopped shallot

1 or 2 chiles, such as Fresno, jalapeño, or cayenne, cut into rings, with seeds intact

The availability of coconut water, which is so popular nowadays, makes this dish possible. It was inspired by a roasted game bird recipe in *Làm Bếp Giỏi*, the Vietnamese equivalent of the *Joy of Cooking*, published in the early 1940s by Van Dai, a Hanoi-born poetess and author. In that recipe, the birds were cooked on the stove top with fresh coconut water until the liquid reduced and coated them with a lovely, mildly sweet flavor.

I applied the technique to boneless, skinless chicken thighs and added coconut oil for richness and fresh chile for zip and color (employ two chiles for a spicy edge). The simple, weeknight dish comes together quickly and reheats splendidly for a leftovers lunch. Serve with rice and sautéed greens (after finishing this dish, throw the greens into the skillet and add a splash of water and/or oil).

/

Cut the chicken thighs into 2-inch pieces and transfer to a large bowl. Add the ginger, cornstarch, salt, caramel sauce, and fish sauce and stir to coat the chicken well. Set aside.

If the coconut water needs an extra hint of sweetness, add sugar by the ¼ teaspoon. Set aside.

In a large nonstick skillet over medium heat, melt 1 tablespoon of the coconut oil. Turn the heat to medium-high, add the chicken, and cook for about 1 minute, until the edges look opaque and the chicken is beginning to brown. Turn the chicken and cook for 45 to 60 seconds more. Add the coconut water and scatter the shallot around the chicken. Bring to a boil and continue boiling for 10 to 12 minutes, turning the chicken occasionally, until there's little to no liquid and you're left with mostly sizzling oil. Add the chiles and cook for 1 minute, stirring constantly, until slightly softened and fragrant. Transfer the chicken and chiles to a bowl.

Splash about 3 tablespoons coconut water into the pan and add the remaining 1½ teaspoons coconut oil. Stir to combine and let bubble for about 30 seconds, until slightly thickened. Pour the sauce over the chicken and chiles (or return them to the pan) and stir to coat. Transfer to a shallow bowl or plate and serve.

CHICKEN, LEMONGRASS, AND sweet potato curry

SERVES 4 TO 6

TAKES ABOUT 45 MINUTES

½ cup coarsely chopped lemongrass (from 2 medium stalks)

2 tablespoons coarsely chopped peeled ginger

1 medium yellow onion, coarsely chopped

2 tablespoons Madras-style curry powder (preferably Sun brand)

½ teaspoon recently ground black pepper

¼ teaspoon cayenne pepper (optional)

One 13½-ounce can full-fat unsweetened coconut milk, unshaken

2 tablespoons virgin coconut oil or neutral oil, such as canola

4 large boneless, skinless chicken thighs (about 1¾ pounds total), each cut into 3 pieces

Fine sea salt

1¼ pounds sweet potatoes, peeled and cut into 1-inch chunks

3 to 5 fresh cilantro sprigs, coarsely chopped

Though Thailand, with its variety of curry pastes, is next door, Viet cooks prefer curry featuring Indian spice blends. The fragrant curry is enriched with coconut milk and served with baguette for dipping or with rice—either plain boiled rice or the vibrant turmeric rice on page 188. Such seamless blending of cultures reflects the unique amalgam that is Vietnam.

This rendition of *cà ri gà* is based on what I grew up with. It's rustic yet elegant, with big lemongrass and ginger notes. Bone-in chicken is typically used, but the curry cooks faster with boneless, skinless thighs. Finishing the curry with thick, rich coconut cream refreshes flavors. It's easy to obtain: let a can of coconut milk sit for a few days (or refrigerate for a few hours), then open and scoop out the fattier cream. The remainder is the thinner, lighter milk. Orange-flesh sweet potatoes easily become mushy, so monitor the pot if you use them. For a more savory result, choose a potato suitable for boiling or roasting, such as red, white, or Yukon gold.

/

In a food processor, whirl the lemongrass into a fine texture, about 3 minutes, pausing occasionally to scrape down the bowl. Add the ginger and pulse to finely chop. Add the onion and pulse again to chop. Add the curry powder, black pepper, and cayenne (if using) and whirl until you have a fragrant yellow paste.

Remove ⅓ cup of the thick cream at the top of the coconut milk, stir the remaining lighter milk, and set both aside.

In a 3- to 4-quart pot over medium-high heat, melt the coconut oil. Add the lemongrass paste and cook for 3 to 5 minutes, stirring frequently, until fragrant and no longer raw and harsh smelling. Lower the heat, as needed, to avoid scorching. Add the chicken and ½ teaspoon salt, stir to combine, and cook for 1 minute to meld the flavors. Add the coconut milk and a little water to cover the chicken. Bring to a simmer over medium-high heat, cover, and adjust the heat to gently simmer for 15 minutes; stirring occasionally.

/ CONTINUED

Uncover the pot, add the sweet potatoes, and return the curry to a simmer. Continue cooking, uncovered, for 10 to 12 minutes, stirring occasionally, until the potatoes are tender. Turn off the heat, add the coconut cream, stirring it into the sauce, and let rest on the burner's receding heat for 10 minutes, uncovered, to blend and mature flavors. Taste and season with salt (unsalted curry powder may require an additional teaspoon) and splash in water if the flavors are too strong.

Serve immediately, garnished with the cilantro.

NOTES /

To divide each chicken thigh into three equal pieces, cut the flat side as one piece, then halve the thicker portion. If large thighs are unavailable, use smaller ones and cut each into two pieces.

Pair the bold curry with a mild vegetable side, such as sauteed chard (pictured opposite). If the curry is too hot, squirt on some lime juice to cut the heat.

HONEY-HOISIN ROAST CHICKEN AND *vegetables*

SERVES 4

TAKES 1½ HOURS

4 garlic cloves, smashed

Chubby 1-inch (1-ounce) section ginger, unpeeled, thinly sliced and smashed

Fine sea salt

1 tablespoon sake, gin, or vodka

1 tablespoon soy sauce

Brimming ⅓ cup honey

1 teaspoon Chinese five-spice powder

6 bone-in, skin-on chicken thighs (about 3 pounds total, preferably air-chilled)

3 tablespoons canola or other neutral oil

½ teaspoon recently ground black pepper

1½ pounds sweet potatoes, unpeeled, scrubbed, and cut into long wedges ¾ to 1 inch thick

12 ounces brussels sprouts, halved lengthwise, or broccoli florets, cut into 2-inch-wide pieces

1½ tablespoons hoisin sauce, plus more as needed

I adore Chinese-style roast duck, with its brown lacquered skin, heady sweet sauce, and fragrant five-spice seasoning. But I rarely have time to prep and air-chill the duck for a couple of days. My default approach is to roast air-chilled chicken thighs, separating the skin from the flesh and brushing on a honey-soy glaze to a shiny, crisp effect. The result is an amazing rendition of *gà quay mật ong* (honey-roasted chicken). To build a meal, I roast vegetables in the oven too. Sweet potatoes and brussels sprouts or broccoli cook on a lower rack while the chicken sizzles above. It's efficient, cozy cooking that is perfect for fall or winter.

/

In a small saucepan over medium heat, combine the garlic, ginger, ¼ teaspoon salt, sake, soy sauce, and honey and bring to a bubbly boil. Remove from the heat and let rest for 5 minutes, then strain the glaze into a heatproof bowl or measuring cup. Set aside.

Line a large rimmed baking sheet with aluminum foil and set a rack inside.

In a small bowl, combine the five-spice powder with 1 teaspoon salt. Rub the seasonings on the flat underside of each chicken thigh, flip the thigh and peel back the skin, and then season the flesh underneath. Reposition the skin and sprinkle ½ teaspoon salt on top. Put the thighs on the prepared rack, spaced as far apart as possible for heat circulation during roasting. For good flavor and crisp skin, let the chicken sit, uncovered, at room temperature for 30 to 45 minutes (the longer the better).

Meanwhile, position racks in the upper and lower thirds of the oven and preheat to 425°F. Line a rimmed baking sheet with parchment paper or aluminum foil.

In a medium bowl, combine the canola oil, pepper, and a rounded ½ teaspoon salt and then toss with the sweet potato and brussels sprouts. Arrange the potatoes, skin-side down, on the prepared baking sheet.

Set aside about ¼ cup of the glaze to use for sauce. The remainder will be used during roasting.

Slide the chicken onto the upper oven rack and the sweet potatoes onto the lower rack and roast for about 40 minutes, checking three times at 10-minute intervals. After the first 10 minutes, brush the glaze all over the skin of the chicken and add the brussels sprouts to the baking sheet with the potatoes. After another 10 minutes, flip the thighs and glaze their undersides. Roast for 10 minutes more to set the glaze, then flip the thighs and brush glaze on the skin. Roast for a final 8 to 10 minutes, until the shiny skin is a rich brown and a meat thermometer inserted into the thickest part of a thigh reaches 160°F.

Remove the chicken from the oven. If the sweet potatoes didn't brown enough, roast on the top rack for 5 to 10 minutes longer. Let the chicken and vegetables rest for 5 to 10 minutes. Mix the reserved glaze with the hoisin sauce; if needed, add up to 1½ teaspoons hoisin to create a pleasant savory-sweet finish.

Transfer the chicken and vegetables to serving plates and serve, passing the hoisin mixture alongside.

NOTES /

When prepping huge sweet potatoes, halve them crosswise first to more easily cut the wedges for this recipe.

Instead of the brussels sprouts or broccoli, use small parsnips, turnips, or sunchokes: scrub and keep the skin intact, then halve the vegetables for roasting.

If the chicken isn't air-chilled, refrigerate the seasoned thighs on the rack, uncovered, overnight or up to 24 hours; let them sit at room temperature for 1 hour before roasting.

The glaze will keep, covered, in the refrigerator, for up to 5 days.

To make your efforts go further, save two thighs (or make extra!) for Roast Chicken Noodle Soup (page 87).

SHRIMP IN coconut caramel sauce

SERVES 4

TAKES 35 MINUTES

1¼ pounds extra-large or jumbo shrimp, peeled and deveined

1⅓ cups coconut water

1½ tablespoons sugar, plus more as needed

1 tablespoon Caramel Sauce (page 32), or 1½ teaspoons molasses

1½ tablespoons fish sauce, plus more as needed

2 tablespoons virgin coconut oil

1 large shallot, halved and sliced

3 large garlic cloves, sliced

Recently ground black pepper

1 green onion, green part only, thinly sliced

My niece Paulina requested this savory-sweet comfort food from southern Vietnam, a region where cooks use coconut milk and coconut water for a sunny array of dishes. I happily obliged because it's delicious and involves a nifty technique—coconut water is reduced with other ingredients until it caramelizes a bit to create a lovely syrupy sauce. Enjoy *tôm rim nước dừa* with rice and a simple vegetable, like the charred brussels sprouts on page 170. Choose a skillet or sauteuse pan (think squat Dutch oven) with a light interior to easily monitor the color changes during cooking.

/

Pat the shrimp with paper towels to remove excess moisture, and set aside.

In a medium bowl, combine the coconut water, sugar, caramel sauce, and fish sauce and stir to mix; taste and make sure it's pleasantly salty-sweet. It will cook down later and intensify but use this opportunity to check the flavor. If needed, add up to 1½ teaspoons sugar or fish sauce, or both. Set aside.

In a large skillet or sauteuse pan over medium heat, melt the coconut oil. When the oil is barely shimmering, add the shallot and garlic and cook, stirring frequently, for 3 to 4 minutes, until the garlic is pale blond. Remove from the heat and, once the cooking action subsides, add the coconut water mixture.

Return the skillet to high heat and bring to a boil. Cook, without stirring, for 10 to 14 minutes, until reduced to between ⅓ and ½ cup (it will have thickened and darkened). Add the shrimp and continue cooking at a swift simmer, stirring frequently, for 3 to 5 minutes, until the shrimp curls up and cooks through and the sauce is slightly syrupy. (Expect the shrimp's natural juices to release, thin out, and flavor the sauce.) If the shrimp cooks too fast, remove it from the pan, let the sauce cook down, and then return the shrimp. Remove from the heat, season with lots of pepper, and stir in the green onion. Let sit for 5 minutes for the flavors to settle and deepen.

Transfer the shrimp to a shallow bowl or plate and serve.

shrimp buying tips

To guarantee great flavor, cook with the best shrimp you can afford. Most shrimp sold at supermarkets have been frozen and thawed. Ask for a little extra if they're not fully thawed (why pay for ice?). If the shrimp doesn't look fresh, ask to smell one. If there's an ammonia scent, pass.

Better yet, buy frozen shrimp and thaw them yourself. At markets where sustainable seafood is sold (such as Whole Foods), purchase large bags of shell-on shrimp that have been individually quick-frozen. Thaw the shrimp, as needed, in a bowl of cold water and pat dry with paper towels before prepping.

Pre-peeled shrimp save time, but they tend to cost more and often have flabby texture and meh flavor. You'll get tasty shrimp if you peel and devein them yourself.

With regard to shrimp sizes, there's plenty of wiggle room. When possible, buy by the count—a numerical range set by the seafood industry of shrimp per 1 pound. If a count is unavailable (look on the package or ask the fishmonger), eyeball the shell-on shrimp at their thickest segment. No ruler handy? Use your fingers as a rough guide. But if your shrimp size is off, don't worry; your dish won't be ruined.

SIZE	COUNT (NUMBER OF SHRIMP PER POUND)	APPROXIMATE WIDTH AT THICKEST SEGMENT
Small	51 to 60 or 61 to 70	½ inch (pinkie width)
Medium	36 to 42 or 43 to 50	⅝ inch (slightly thicker than a pinkie)
Large	26 to 30 or 31 to 35	¾ inch (middle-finger width)
Extra-large	21 to 25	⅞ inch (width at base of index finger)
Jumbo	16 to 20	1 inch (thumb at its widest)

POMEGRANATE SRIRACHA shrimp

SERVES 4

TAKES 15 MINUTES

1½ pounds extra-large or
jumbo shrimp, peeled and
deveined

Fine sea salt

2 teaspoons sriracha,
plus more as needed

2 tablespoons pomegranate
molasses (see page 34)

2 tablespoons fish sauce

3½ tablespoons water

1½ teaspoons to
1½ tablespoons packed
light or dark brown sugar

1 teaspoon cornstarch

2 tablespoons canola or
other neutral oil

1 shallot, finely chopped

2 garlic cloves, finely chopped

3 or 4 sprigs fresh cilantro

Tangy, salty, and spicy tamarind shrimp is a southern Viet favorite, but tamarind isn't available yet at many supermarkets. My work-around is to use pomegranate molasses for the sauce base. It totally works with the fish sauce and chile heat to create a quick modern take on a Vietnamese classic. Enjoy the shrimp with rice for soaking up the sauce. They're also good tucked into a warm corn tortilla or plopped atop grits. To feature tamarind instead of pomegranate, substitute tamarind liquid, concentrate, or paste; see page 35 for details.

/

Refresh the shrimp by putting them in a colander and tossing them with about ¼ teaspoon salt. Rinse immediately under cold water and drain, then pat with paper towel to remove excess moisture. Set aside.

In a small bowl, combine the sriracha, pomegranate molasses, fish sauce, and 3 tablespoons of the water. Taste and add the brown sugar, starting with 1½ teaspoons, to create a tart sweetness; the amount you need depends on the tartness of the pomegranate molasses and your palate. For extra heat, add more sriracha, ½ teaspoon at a time. (I typically end up with 1 tablespoon total. Make a note after settling on your preferred heat level.) Aim for a tangy, savory, spicy finish. Set the sauce aside. In a small bowl or cup, stir the cornstarch with the remaining 1½ teaspoons water, then set the slurry aside.

In a large skillet over high heat, warm the canola oil until hot but not smoking. Add the shallot and garlic and stir-fry for about 30 seconds, until fragrant. Add the shrimp and stir-fry for about 1 minute, until most of them have turned pinkish orange and are slightly curled.

Give the sauce a stir, then add to the pan, stirring to combine. Let the sauce come to a vigorous boil, stirring occasionally to keep things moving. When the shrimp are cooked through, about 2 minutes, give the cornstarch slurry a stir and add to the pan. Cook, stirring, to slightly thicken the sauce and coat the shrimp.

Transfer the shrimp to a deep plate or shallow bowl and garnish with the cilantro. Serve immediately.

VIET-CAJUN seafood boil

SERVES 4 TO 6

TAKES 45 MINUTES

1 pound small "new" potatoes

1 head garlic, papery skin
  removed if there is a thick
  layer of it

12 cups water

2 tablespoons Old Bay
  seasoning, or your favorite
  seafood boil seasoning
  blend, plus 1¼ teaspoons

Fine sea salt

1 medium orange or lemon

3 medium ears corn, husked,
  and cut crosswise into
  4 sections

8 ounces andouille or
  kielbasa sausage, cut into
  1½- to 2-inch chunks

1⅓ pounds extra-large or
  jumbo shrimp, snipped
  along the back of the shell
  with scissors and deveined

10 ounces mussels

6 tablespoons butter

¾ teaspoon cayenne pepper

¾ teaspoon recently
  ground black pepper or
  white pepper

1 or 2 limes, cut into wedges

During the 1980s, my uncle Thao regularly gifted our family with crawfish that he caught near his home in Southern California. We'd never seen the tiny lobster-like creatures but were undaunted: Viet people adore picking through piles of shellfish and crustaceans to savor the bits of flesh with *muối tiêu chanh* (salt, pepper, and lime dipping sauce). It's a fun way to nosh, fueled by conversation and beer.

Decades later, I found myself researching Viet-Cajun crawfish boils for the Southern Foodways Alliance. These popular boils entailed coating the cooked components in a heady sauce of spices, garlic, and butter or margarine. When I interviewed Dada Ngo, the co-owner of Boiling Crab, a successful chain founded in California with roots in Houston and the Texas Gulf fishing community, she didn't share her sauce recipe but offered this: Flavor your boil however you want—what's key is using the best seafood possible in your locale. Live crawfish is rare where I live, so I use shrimp and mussels for my California take on a culinary mash-up that could only happen in America. Boils are easy; you just add the various components to the pot at intervals so they don't overcook. Add a lightly dressed green salad for a balanced meal.

/

In an 8-quart stockpot, combine the potatoes, garlic, water, 2 tablespoons Old Bay, and 1 teaspoon salt and set over high heat.

Finely grate the orange zest directly into a small saucepan. Set aside.

Halve the zested citrus, then squeeze the juice directly into the stockpot. Cover the pot and bring to a boil. Uncover and boil for 8 to 10 minutes, until the potatoes are halfway cooked (a knife tip easily penetrates ½ inch before meeting resistance). Set the corn, sausage, shrimp, and mussels nearby.

Remove the head of garlic from the pot, transfer to a plate, and let cool for a few minutes. Add the corn to the pot, return the water to a boil, and cook for 3 to 5 minutes, until the potatoes are tender (easily pierced with a knife to the center).

/ CONTINUED

Meanwhile, trim the root end from the garlic and slip the skins off the cloves; it's okay if they're not totally tender. Put the garlic through a press (or chop and mash with a knife) and let the results fall into the saucepan with the zest. Add the butter, cayenne, and remaining 1¼ teaspoons Old Bay and cook over medium-low heat for about 2 minutes to melt the butter and meld flavors; the garlic should be distinct but not raw and strong. Set aside to cool.

After the corn and potatoes are cooked through, add the sausage and shrimp to the boil, then top with the mussels. Cover the pot and let the shellfish poach for 2 minutes (there's no need to bring to a boil), until the mussels have opened and the shrimp have curled and turned pink. Remove the pot from the heat, uncover, and stir 2 to 3 tablespoons of the cooking liquid into the garlic butter.

Set a large colander in the sink, then pour the pot of boiled ingredients into it to drain. Return half of the boiled ingredients to the pot, pour in half of the garlic butter, stir with a large spoon to coat, and then dump onto a rimmed baking sheet. Repeat with the rest of the boil. Combine the black pepper and 1 teaspoon salt and divide among individual small dishes.

Bring the boil to the table to serve. Invite diners to make their own sauce by squeezing lime juice over the salt and pepper and stirring it together. Don't forget paper towels for easy cleanup.

NOTES /

Boiling the garlic mellows it, for a more elegant flavor.

Instead of mussels, use small clams, adding them when the potatoes are nearly tender, since they need more time to open than mussels. Small Dungeness or regular-size blue or stone crabs may stand in for some of the seafood too; add them after the potatoes have cooked for about 5 minutes. You may omit the sausage and mussels and increase the quantity of shrimp to 2 pounds.

No small potatoes? Buy large ones and cut them into 1½- to 2-inch chunks.

If you use a raw sausage, cook it fully before adding other ingredients.

Without a large colander to strain the boil, use tongs and a spider skimmer to retrieve the cooked items from the pot.

For another tasty dip, stir together 3 tablespoons mayonnaise, 1½ tablespoons ketchup, and ¼ teaspoon recently ground black pepper. Adjust the flavors for fatty, tangy, and mildly spicy results. Make the sauce as the boil cooks and set at the table. Let diners dip their food directly into the sauce.

GINGER-GARLIC FISH parcels

SERVES 4

TAKES 25 MINUTES

3 garlic cloves, thinly sliced

¼ cup thin, matchstick-cut ginger

1¼ teaspoons sugar

¼ teaspoon recently ground black pepper

2 tablespoons oyster sauce

2 tablespoons soy sauce

2 tablespoons canola or other neutral oil, plus more for brushing

8 ounces baby bok choy, quartered and cut on a sharp diagonal into pieces about 1 inch wide and 2 inches long

1½ teaspoons toasted sesame oil

One 1⅓-pound salmon or halibut fillet, about 1 inch thick at the center

2 medium green onions, green and white parts, cut on a sharp diagonal into pieces about 2 inches long

When you don't have a traditional Chinese steamer for steaming fish, take a cue from the French and bake it in parchment paper. The *en papillote* method keeps fish moist, the way steaming does, making it great for seafood-shy cooks! Plus, it's incredibly easy and fun. Each person gets their own packet to open up and release the fragrant vapors. I like to put my rice into the packet to let it soak up all the sauce.

A one-inch-thick salmon or halibut fillet works splendidly here. When baby bok choy (the Shanghai variety is popular at stores) is unavailable, use napa cabbage or a similar moisture-rich leafy green vegetable. Of the many ways to cut the paper, heart shapes fold up neatly for the parcels. Plus, they're romantic.

/

Position racks in the upper and lower thirds of the oven and pre-heat to 375°F. Cut four pieces of parchment paper, each about 15 by 24 inches. Fold each one over to form a 15 by 12-inch rectangle. Draw a large half of a heart on each one, so its straight edge is on the fold. Use scissors to cut them out. Set aside.

In a small bowl, combine the garlic, ginger, sugar, pepper, oyster sauce, soy sauce, and canola oil. In a larger bowl, toss the bok choy with the sesame oil. Set the seasonings and bok choy aside. Cut the salmon crosswise into four equal pieces.

Unfold each parchment-paper heart and brush the insides with canola oil, leaving a dry 3-inch border. Divide the bok choy among the hearts, putting it on one side, then top with some white parts of green onion. Place a piece of salmon on top. Top each piece of fish with one-fourth of the seasonings. Scatter on the remaining green onion. Bring the empty side of each parchment heart over the fish and line up the edges. Starting from the top of the heart, fold the edges over about ½ inch, working with roughly 1½ inches at a time. Press the creases down so they hold. When done, twist the pointy bottom of each heart to finish. Transfer the parcels to two large

/ CONTINUED

rimmed baking sheets. (At this point, the parcels may be refrigerated for up to 2 hours. Return them to room temperature before baking.)

Bake the fish for 8 minutes, then rotate and swap the baking sheets and bake for another 6 to 7 minutes, until the parcels have puffed.

Serve the fish immediately, letting diners cut open the parcels themselves.

NOTES /

No patience for paper? Bake in foil. Use rectangular pieces about 12 inches wide and 16 inches long. With one of the shorter sides facing you, oil the foil as directed, then arrange the ingredients below the midline. Fold the top half of the foil over the fish to meet the edge of the foil close to you. Fold the edges over and bake as directed.

Extra tweaks to consider: If ginger matchsticks don't appeal, peel and finely grate a 1½-inch section of ginger. Instead of brushing oil on the parchment paper, use an oil sprayer. Include two thinly sliced fresh shiitake mushrooms for extra interest.

If halving this recipe (say, for date night), bake in the middle of a 400°F oven for 12 to 14 minutes (no need to rotate the pan), until the parchment paper puffs up.

CRISPY LEMONGRASS *salmon*

SERVES 4

TAKES 1 HOUR

1½ tablespoons chopped lemongrass (from 1 medium stalk)

1½ teaspoons packed light or dark brown sugar

Fine sea salt

2 tablespoons chopped shallot

1½ teaspoons fish sauce, plus more as needed

½ teaspoon Madras-style curry powder (preferably Sun brand)

1 tablespoon canola or other neutral oil, plus more as needed

One 1⅓-pound skin-on salmon fillet, about 1 inch thick at the center

We never had salmon in Vietnam, but once my family tasted it in America, we adopted it as if it were native to Vietnam. We prepared it in various ways; this recipe employs a piquant paste of lemongrass, shallot, and curry that Older Sister Thien, our cook in Saigon, used to spread on whole fish destined to be grilled over charcoal. My mom re-created the mixture, applied it to a salmon fillet, and broiled the fish to a wonderful crispness. Slitting the fish through its skin allows the seasonings to penetrate faster. Enjoy the salmon with rice or feature it in a rice noodle salad (see Note, page 199). If you're new to prepping lemongrass, see the tips on page 156.

/

In a small food processor, combine the lemongrass, brown sugar, and ¼ teaspoon salt and grind until the lemongrass is minced. Add the shallot, fish sauce, curry powder, and canola oil and run the machine, pausing to scrape down the sides, until you have a coarse paste. Taste the seasoning paste. You want it a little saltier than you're comfortable with, so if needed, add more salt, a pinch at a time, or fish sauce in ½-teaspoon increments. Set aside.

Cut the salmon crosswise into four equal portions, then make two ¼-inch-deep, 2-inch-long slits, about ½ inch apart, on the skin side of each piece of fish. Rub the seasoning paste all over the fish and into the slits. Cover with plastic wrap and set aside at room temperature for 30 to 45 minutes.

Meanwhile, position a rack 5 to 6 inches from the broiler element and set the oven to broil. Let it heat up for about 15 minutes, so it's really hot. Cover a baking sheet with aluminum foil and set a rack inside.

Drizzle the fish with canola oil and arrange the pieces, skin-side up, on the prepared rack. Broil for 2 to 3 minutes, until the skin is slightly charred. Use a metal spatula to flip the fish and then broil for about 3 minutes, until the flesh no longer looks raw and is beginning to brown. If you don't like crisp skin, broil the flesh side for about 1 minute longer, to darken and pick up character. If you like crispy skin, flip the fish so the skin is up. Broil for 30 to 60 seconds longer to crisp the skin. Monitor carefully to avoid super-blackened skin. Remove from the oven and let rest for 5 minutes before serving.

GRILLED TROUT rice paper rolls

SERVES 4

TAKES ABOUT 45 MINUTES

RICH GREEN ONIONS

3 tablespoons neutral oil, or 2 tablespoons neutral oil plus 1 tablespoon toasted sesame oil

¾ cup thinly sliced green onion, white and green parts

Fine sea salt

6 ounces small dried round rice noodles (maifun), or 8 ounces dried rice capellini

2 or 3 whole cleaned, gutted trout (about 2¼ pounds total)

About 2 tablespoons canola or other neutral oil

Fine sea salt and recently ground black pepper

¼ cup fried onions or shallots (optional)

1 cup Nuoc Cham Dipping Sauce (page 30)

Leaves from 1 head soft-leaf lettuce (such as butter, Boston, or red or green leaf), or 4 to 5 cups gently packed baby lettuce

1 small handful fresh mint, basil, or other soft-leaf fresh herbs (except cilantro)

1 small handful fresh cilantro

24 rice papers, each 8 inches wide

One of my favorite easy summertime meals is to buy whole trout, season it simply, and have my husband grill it to a crisp. While he's outside, I'm setting out the ingredients for a roll-your-own meal of lettuce and rice paper wraps. The noodles were boiled earlier in the day (or maybe even days before), and the lettuce, herbs, dipping sauce, and rich green onions were prepared in advance too. When I'm short on time, I omit the green onions (*mỡ hành*, which means "fatty onion" in Vietnamese) and substitute store-bought fried onions. To go over the top, I offer both.

My husband brings in the cooked fish and we start our leisurely meal, fashioning rice paper rolls with all the accoutrements. We compete to see who rolls the handsomest ones, and laugh when an overstuffed roll busts. We sip on beer or wine while waiting for the rice paper to soften. It's a perfect Vietnamese one-dish meal, which can be enjoyed as a light lunch or dinner. Details on rice paper and a roll-your-own tutorial are on page 42.

/

To make the rich green onions In a small saucepan over medium heat, warm the oil until hot (a green onion slice should sizzle on contact). Add the green onion and a large pinch of salt and stir. When the green onion has softened, about 30 seconds, remove the pan from the heat. Transfer the pan's contents to a small heatproof bowl and let cool completely, about 15 minutes, before using. (Cover and keep for up to 3 hours at room temperature or refrigerate for up to 7 days.)

Meanwhile, in a pot of unsalted water, boil the noodles until chewy-tender; the cooking time depends on the noodle and brand. Drain in a colander, rinse with cold water, and drain well. Set aside or transfer to an airtight container and refrigerate for up to 3 days.

Rinse the trout well and pat dry with paper towels. Using a sharp knife, make crosswise slits, at a 45- to 60-degree angle and ¼ to ½ inch deep, on both sides of the belly in three or four places per side, spacing them about 1¼ inches apart. Rub the canola oil inside and outside each fish. Season the cavity and skin with salt and pepper. Set aside.

/ CONTINUED

Prepare a medium charcoal fire or preheat a gas grill to medium (you can hold your hand 6 inches above the grill for 4 to 5 seconds) and lightly oil the grate.

Place the trout on the grate and grill for 4 to 6 minutes on each side, until the skin is crisp and browned here and there. Using two metal spatulas, or one metal spatula plus tongs or a carving fork, nudge one spatula under the fish to loosen it from the grate and use the other tool to assist in the flip. (If the skin sticks, it's usually the first side. By the time you turn the fish, it's cooked enough that the second side doesn't stick. Present the prettier side up.) The trout is ready when the meat is opaque. Peek inside the cavity; there should be no sign of blood. Transfer the fish to a platter and, if you like, decorate each with a little of the rich green onion (include the oil) and fried onions and place on the table.

If needed, soften and refresh the noodles by sprinkling with water and microwaving on high for 60 to 90 seconds. Since the noodles are unwieldy, arrange them as twenty-four nests on two plates or in low bowls. Set on the table with the dipping sauce. Arrange the lettuce, herbs, and cilantro on one or two platters, and the rice paper on another. Set each place with a dinner plate, a small bowl for the dipping sauce, and chopsticks or a fork and a spoon. Put out two shallow bowls filled with 1 to 2 inches of very warm water for softening the rice papers.

For each roll, slide a rice paper round in the warm water for a few seconds to wet both sides, then place on a dinner plate. When the rice paper is pliable and tacky, about 1 minute, arrange the ingredients in the lower third—a lettuce leaf (or small handful of baby lettuce), some torn herb leaves, a noodle portion, and some fish (with or without skin). If desired, top with the rich green onions and flavorful oil and some fried onions. Drizzle in a little sauce, or spoon it in while eating the roll. Regardless, close up the rice paper and enjoy.

GREEN ONION BASICS

In Vietnamese, green onions are called *hành lá* ("onion with leaves"). The hollow, dark green parts are technically the plant's shoots. They're milder in flavor than the more solid bulb stalk, which is lighter in color. Green onions, along with regular onions, leafy greens, and cilantro, have quercetin, an antioxidant that may help fight heart disease, diabetes, and rheumatoid arthritis.

In my recipes, the "white part" of the green onion refers to the solid part, which is pale green to white. Its bolder, harsher flavor makes it better for cooking than as a raw garnish, especially when new friends are over.

Most green onion prep requires slicing the onion crosswise into rings; you can keep the rings in an airtight container for up to 2 days.

Need chopped green onion? Cut an onion into 4-inch sections, then use the tip of your knife to halve the pieces lengthwise. Cut crosswise and then, as needed, use a rocking motion to chop into smaller pieces. Chopped green onion gets mushy when refrigerated. Use it soon after prep.

5

Celebrate meat in simply delicious
and resourceful Vietnamese ways.
From glazed and grilled to fried and
braised, these recipes offer some of
my all-time favorites, dishes that
I've adored from childhood into
adulthood.

PORK AND beef

HONEY-GLAZED pork riblets

SERVES 4

TAKES ABOUT 45 MINUTES

5 garlic cloves, coarsely
    chopped

Brimming ⅓ cup coarsely
    chopped shallot

1½ teaspoons Chinese
    five-spice powder

1 teaspoon packed light
    or dark brown sugar

½ teaspoon fine sea salt

Rounded ¼ teaspoon
    recently ground
    black pepper

1½ tablespoons fish sauce

One 2½- to 3-pound slab
    St. Louis–style pork ribs,
    sawed through the bone
    into 2 long strips

3 tablespoons honey

1½ teaspoons sriracha

Serving someone a whole slab of ribs is not a Viet thing. People love to nibble and gnaw on small riblets, which cook up fast and take on the seasonings well (there's more surface area exposed).

When I have a hankering for Viet-style ribs but am short on time, I use the pressure cooker to quickly steam them to tenderness and then broil them with a light sweet-spicy glaze. I buy a slab of St. Louis-style ribs (they've been trimmed of the thick, cartilage-laden rib tips) and ask the butcher to saw it in half through the bone into two long strips. In about 45 minutes, I have a pile of ribs to offer as finger food, serve on a rice plate, or pair with mango and jicama salad (see page 163) and a potato salad. If you don't have a pressure cooker, cook the ribs in the oven (see the Notes).

/

Pour 1 cup water into a 6-quart pressure cooker or multicooker. Set a metal steamer basket (use a perforated metal insert designed for a pressure cooker or a large collapsible steamer basket) inside the cooker. Set aside.

In a small food processor, combine the garlic, shallot, five-spice powder, brown sugar, salt, pepper, and 1 tablespoon of the fish sauce and whirl together, pausing to scrape down the sides and add ½ teaspoon water if needed. (If you don't have a processor, mince the garlic and shallot and then combine with the other ingredients.) Transfer the marinade to a large bowl.

Halve each rib strip between two bones so they're more manageable. Add to the marinade and use your fingers to coat well.

Put the ribs in the prepared pressure cooker, arranging them in the steamer basket somewhat loosely to facilitate even cooking. (I stand the strips like a tepee or coil them.) Lock the lid in place. Bring to high pressure, adjust the heat to maintain pressure, and cook for 15 minutes. Then, remove from the heat, depressurize naturally for 10 minutes, and release the residual pressure. (If using a multi-cooker, program it to cook at high pressure for 15 minutes—*do not*

/ CONTINUED

use the steam function—then turn it off or unplug it and depressurize for 15 minutes before releasing residual pressure.)

While the cooker depressurizes, set an oven rack in the middle position and preheat the broiler, so it's nice and hot. Line a rimmed baking sheet with aluminum foil and place a rack inside.

In a small bowl, stir together the honey, sriracha, and remaining 1½ teaspoons fish sauce. Set the glaze aside.

Unlock the cooker and, using tongs, place the ribs, bone-side up, on the prepared pan. Brush the ribs with some of the honey glaze, then broil for 4 to 5 minutes, until sizzling and browned here and there. Flip the ribs and repeat the glazing and broiling. Remove from the oven and let cool for a few minutes, then brush on any remaining glaze for extra shine. Cut between the bones.

Serve the ribs hot, warm, or at room temperature.

NOTES /

To steam the ribs in a pressure cooker larger than 6 quarts, add water to a depth of a good ¼ inch.

Instead of finishing the ribs in the oven, grill them outdoors.

The cooked, unglazed ribs will keep in the refrigerator for up to 3 days. Bring to room temperature, bake at 400°F on a prepared baking sheet and rack for 12 minutes to reheat, and then glaze and broil for 5 to 6 minutes per side.

Instead of pressure cooking the ribs, bake them. For the most even and efficient cooking, bake the ribs in pairs in two foil packets. Arrange the rib strips side by side on the foil, and wrap each of the two packages completely. Set them on a rimmed baking sheet and cook in a 350°F oven for 1¼ to 1½ hours. Let cool for about 10 minutes, unwrap, and finish by glazing and broiling.

DOWN-HOME PANFRIED pork cutlets

SERVES 4

TAKES 45 MINUTES

1⅓ pounds thin-cut boneless pork loin chops, each about ⅓ inch thick

2 large garlic cloves, put through a press or minced and mashed

½ teaspoon fine sea salt

¼ teaspoon recently ground black pepper

1 teaspoon fish sauce or soy sauce

½ cup fine yellow cornmeal or plain bread crumbs

Canola or other neutral oil for panfrying

Chile garlic sauce (see page 31) for serving

Bragg Liquid Aminos, Maggi Seasoning sauce, or soy sauce for serving

This unpretentious recipe dates back to 1944, when my mom first had it in Hai Duong, the town where she grew up. The original, *thịt cốt lết*, was made with beef, but since beef was a luxury item, Mom's brother-in-law taught her how to make the dish with affordable pork. He seasoned it just like a beefsteak and quickly fried it up. It was delicious, and when Mom came to America and discovered supermarket bread crumbs, she began breading pork cutlets and panfrying them, much to our family's delight. (The term *cốt lết* comes from *côtelette*, which is French for "cutlet" or "chop.")

My updated recipe includes cornmeal, a gluten-free, crunchy coating option. If boneless chops are unavailable, use deboned pork shoulder (blade) steak of similar thickness. For a satisfying meal, serve with rice and roasted cauliflower, or steamed vegetables, or a green salad.

/

Use paper towel to blot excess moisture from the pork. Using a meat mallet or the spine of a knife, gently pound and tenderize each pork chop. Set aside.

In a small bowl, combine the garlic, salt, pepper, and fish sauce and mix to make a paste. Rub the paste all over the pork, then cover and set aside to marinate at room temperature for 30 minutes.

Put the cornmeal on a plate. Add the marinated pork chops to the cornmeal and coat each chop. Set aside.

In a large skillet over medium-high heat, add enough oil to film the bottom. In batches, panfry the pork for 4 to 5 minutes, turning at about the 2½-minute mark, when the first side is golden brown. The second side will not fry up evenly, so let your best efforts be on the first. Between batches, add a little more oil, if needed, and use a spoon to remove some of the dark cornmeal that inevitably accumulates. Transfer the cooked pieces to a rack to rest while you panfry the remaining pork.

Serve the pork with its more handsome side up, either hot or warm, with chile garlic sauce and liquid aminos for dipping and swiping. This is knife-and-fork food.

GRILLED LEMONGRASS pork chops

SERVES 4

TAKES 45 MINUTES

MARINADE

3 garlic cloves, roughly chopped

2 tablespoons coarsely chopped shallot, or 3 tablespoons roughly chopped yellow onion

¼ cup coarsely chopped fresh lemongrass (from 2 medium stalks)

2 tablespoons light or dark brown sugar

Rounded ¼ teaspoon recently ground black pepper

1½ tablespoons canola or other neutral oil

1½ tablespoons fish sauce

1¼ teaspoons soy sauce

½ teaspoon molasses, dark amber honey, or Caramel Sauce (page 32)

4 thin-cut bone-in pork chops (about 6 ounces each), about ½ inch thick

½ cup Nuoc Cham Dipping Sauce (page 30; optional)

Vietnamese cooks love thin pork chops because the chops pick up seasonings quickly, cook fast, and taste great—perfect for a weeknight meal. Sold at many supermarkets, the skinny chops have either a curved rib bone or T-shaped bone. An edge of fat and marbling signal good flavor. You can marinate the pork many ways, but lemongrass is a signature Viet flavor.

Serve these chops with rice and grilled vegetables; season the veggies with leftover marinade, salt, pepper, and oil and then add to the grill. Add a side of pickle (see page 29) for tangy crunch. To make the marinade without a food processor, mince the garlic and shallot, transfer to a large bowl, and mix with 3 tablespoons grated or minced lemongrass (or lemongrass paste) and the remaining ingredients.

/

To make the marinade In a small food processor, combine the garlic, shallot, lemongrass, brown sugar, and pepper and whirl to a fine texture. Add the canola oil, fish sauce, soy sauce, and molasses and process until relatively smooth, like a wet paste. Transfer to a medium bowl.

Use paper towel to blot excess moisture from the pork. Add the pork to the marinade, turning to coat well, then cover and set aside to marinate at room temperature for 30 minutes. Or, refrigerate for up to 24 hours; let the meat sit out at room temperature for 30 minutes before grilling.

Warm a cast-iron stove-top grill pan over medium-high heat, prepare a medium-hot charcoal fire, or preheat a gas grill to medium-high (you can hold your hand 6 inches above the grill for 3 to 4 seconds). Grill the pork chops for 5 to 7 minutes, turning frequently, until firm and cooked through. Pierce with the sharp point of a knife to test (it's okay if the center is faintly pink). Transfer to a plate and let rest for 5 to 10 minutes.

Serve the chops warm, passing the dipping sauce at the table, if desired.

Sauté function on the Instant Pot). Add enough of the canola oil to film the bottom of the pot. When the oil is shimmering, in two or three batches, add the pork and lightly sear on all sides, about 1 minute; transfer the seared pork to a bowl or plate.

Turn off the heat and add all the pork, the caramel sauce, fish sauce, onion, garlic, black peppercorns (with star anise, if using), and coconut water. Lock the lid in place. Bring to high pressure, adjust the heat to maintain pressure, and cook for 12 minutes. Then, remove from the heat, depressurize naturally for 10 minutes, and release the residual pressure. (If using a multicooker, program it to cook at high pressure for 12 minutes, turn it off or unplug it, and depressurize naturally for 15 minutes before releasing residual pressure.)

Unlock the cooker and, using tongs, transfer the pork to a clean bowl or plate, and tent with aluminum foil to prevent it from drying out. If peppercorns cling to the pork, leave them on for zing, if you wish.

Line a mesh strainer with a double layer of paper towels and set the strainer over a large heatproof measuring cup or bowl. Pour the cooking liquid through the strainer. After most of the liquid has passed through and a layer of clear fat remains above the solids, set the strainer aside to continue draining the fat, which you may save for cooking, if you like.

Return the cooking liquid to the cooker and boil over high heat for 15 to 18 minutes, until reduced to about 1 cup, then adjust the heat to a simmer. (If using a multicooker, use a high-heat setting to bring to a boil, then turn off the machine to lower the heat level, if needed.) Add the pork and eggs and cook for 3 to 5 minutes, gently stirring now and then, to heat through and coat them with the dark sauce. Turn off the heat and let rest for 5 minutes, uncovered, to concentrate the flavors. Taste and, if needed, add up to 1½ teaspoons more fish sauce or sugar, or both, to intensify and create a pleasant savory-sweet finish.

Transfer the pork and eggs to a shallow bowl. For spicy heat, ladle some of the sauce into small dishes and muddle the chiles with the sauce so that diners can drizzle it onto their dish.

NOTES /

For variety, combine pork shoulder with belly in a 2:1 ratio.

To steam the eggs in a pressure cooker larger than 6 quarts, add water to a depth of a good ¼ inch.

If you add the eggs to the sauce before adding the pork, they'll pick up darker color and more flavor, but they may turn a bit rubbery, which some people don't mind.

This dish intensifies in flavor as it sits, so make it 1 or 2 days ahead and store, covered, in the refrigerator.

Extend leftovers with chicken stock or broth, and add chopped or thinly sliced vegetables (try bok choy, celery, or carrot) and instant ramen for a quick noodle-soup meal.

To cook this recipe without a pressure cooker, put the eggs in a saucepan with enough water to cover by 1 inch and then boil for 7 to 9 minutes. Cool in an ice bath for 5 to 10 minutes before peeling. Meanwhile, sear the pork in a 3- or 4-quart saucepan, add the remaining ingredients, except the sugar and chiles, and bring to a boil over high heat. Skim the inevitable scum, turn the heat to medium-low, cover, and simmer for 1¼ hours, until the tip of a sharp knife inserted ¼ inch into a chunk of pork meets little resistance. Remove the pork and strain the cooking liquid. Return the liquid to the pan, bring to a boil, and cook for about 5 minutes to reduce it to 1 cup. Continue as directed.

Didn't make caramel sauce in advance? In a small stainless-steel saucepan over medium heat, combine 1 tablespoons water, ⅛ teaspoon distilled or unseasoned rice vinegar, and ¼ cup sugar and stir until the sugar is nearly dissolved, 60 to 90 seconds. Cook for 3 minutes, without stirring, until it is champagne yellow, then continue cooking for another 1 to 2 minutes, frequently picking up the pan and swirling the sauce to control the caramelization process. When it's a dark tea color (expect faint smoke to rise), turn off the heat and keep the pan on the burner. Let the sugar continue caramelizing on the burner's residual heat for 1 to 2 minutes, until it resembles Pinot Noir in color. Remove from the heat and add 2 to 3 tablespoons water; the sugar will seize up, so stir to loosen and dissolve the sugar. If needed, rewarm over medium heat. Scrape into the cooker or pot to combine with the pork.

SHAKING beef

SERVES 4

TAKES 30 MINUTES

MARINATED BEEF

1½ teaspoons sugar

1½ teaspoons cornstarch

½ teaspoon recently ground
black pepper

2 garlic cloves, put through a
press or minced and mashed

1½ to 2 tablespoons
oyster sauce

1 tablespoon soy sauce

1 teaspoon fish sauce

1½ pounds beefsteak, such
as bottom sirloin (tri-tip) or
New York strip, trimmed and
cut into ¾- to 1-inch cubes

1 to 2 tablespoons canola oil

SALAD

¼ cup thinly sliced red onion
or shallot

1½ teaspoons sugar or honey

2 pinches fine sea salt

About 4 grinds black pepper

1½ tablespoons unseasoned
rice vinegar

2 tablespoons water

4 cups lightly packed
watercress, baby arugula,
or other salad greens

¼ cup fresh mint, basil, or
other herb leaves, torn
(optional)

6 to 8 cherry tomatoes,
halved (optional)

A deliciously quirky combo of warm cubes of seared steak atop a cool salad, this classic is traditionally considered a special-occasion dish in Vietnam, where beefsteak is a luxury. Given that, cooks cleverly cut the meat into smaller pieces to imbue it with flavor, cook it quickly, and serve it to a crowd. The name in Vietnamese, *thịt bò lúc lắc*, refers to the back-and-forth shaking (*lúc lắc*) of the skillet as the beef (*thịt bò*) cooks. Shaking beef is a Viet restaurant favorite, and a cinch to make at home.

For the steak, choose well-marbled pieces. When the beef hits the greens, they wilt slightly and the beef juices and dressing blend together into a tangy sauce, which is great spooned over rice or other grains.

/

To prepare the beef In a medium bowl, stir together the sugar, cornstarch, pepper, garlic, 1½ tablespoons of the oyster sauce, the soy sauce, and fish sauce. Taste and, if a saltier finish is needed, add up to 1½ teaspoons oyster sauce. Add the beef, toss to coat well, and let marinate for 20 minutes at room temperature. Keep the canola oil nearby.

To make the salad Rinse the onion in a strainer under cold running water for about 10 seconds, then set aside. In a large bowl (suitable for tossing the salad), whisk together the sugar, salt, pepper, vinegar, and water. Add the onion, top with the watercress, and, if you wish, add the mint and tomatoes, but *don't* toss.

Set a large skillet that can get very hot (such as carbon steel or cast iron) over high heat and add enough of the canola oil to film the bottom. When the oil is shimmering, carefully add the beef, spreading it out in one layer, and cook for 3 to 4 minutes, shaking the pan every 30 to 60 seconds to sear the beef on all sides; it should be medium-rare. (If you want to minimize mess, cover the pan with a splatter guard, and flip the meat with a spatula.) Remove from the heat.

Quickly toss the salad and transfer everything, including the dressing, to a platter or serving dish. Pile the cooked beef and its juices on top, and serve immediately. At the table, ceremoniously combine all the ingredients and invite diners to dive in.

CURRY-SCENTED GRILLED BEEF lettuce wraps

SERVES 4

TAKES ABOUT 45 MINUTES

Brimming ⅓ cup unsalted roasted peanuts or cashews, finely chopped

3 medium green onions, white and green parts, finely chopped

1 tablespoon Madras-style curry powder (preferably Sun brand)

¾ teaspoon recently ground black pepper

3 tablespoons water

Brimming 1 tablespoon oyster sauce

1 tablespoon fish sauce

1½ pounds ground beef (85% lean)

6 ounces small dried round rice noodles (maifun), or 8 ounces dried rice capellini or thin spaghetti (see page 15)

1 cup Nuoc Cham Dipping Sauce (page 30)

Leaves from 1 large head of soft-leaf lettuce (such as butter, Boston, or red or green leaf)

6 to 8 bushy sprigs fresh mint or basil

10 to 12 sprigs fresh cilantro

Making lettuce-and-herb wraps filled with well-seasoned grilled morsels is a quintessential Viet way to eat. It's fun and healthful too. This recipe was inspired by beef wrapped in wild betel leaf (*bò nướng lá lốt*), a favorite. Plentiful in Vietnam but rare outside of Little Saigon markets in America, the heart-shaped, edible leaves magically release a peppery, incense-like aroma during cooking. I conjure up the leaf by seasoning the meat with curry powder, fish sauce, oyster sauce, and lots of black pepper.

Good ground beef, the kind you'd make excellent burgers with, is perfect. Peanuts lend texture, and the water hydrates to prevent a dry finish. With the rice noodles, you have a one-dish meal; but skip them for a low-carb dish. To make a beef rice bowl, see the Notes.

/

In a medium bowl, combine the peanuts, green onions, curry powder, pepper, water, oyster sauce, and fish sauce. Add the beef and mix with your fingers. (If not cooking right away, cover and refrigerate for up to 24 hours.) Form into twenty-four patties, each a good 2 inches wide and ½ inch thick. Set aside.

In large pot of unsalted water, boil the noodles, then drain, rinse with water, drain, and let cool for 5 minutes. Since the noodles are unwieldy, arrange them as 2-inch nests on a plate or in a shallow bowl. Set at the table with the dipping sauce, lettuce, and fresh herbs.

Lightly oil a cast-iron stove-top grill (or lightly film a heavy skillet with oil) and set over medium-high heat. In batches, add the beef and cook for 4 to 5 minutes, turning midway, until medium to medium-well done. (These are usually not eaten medium-rare, but you can cook for less time, if you like.) Transfer to a platter and let cool for a few minutes.

Have diners build lettuce wraps with herbs, noodles, and beef (for easier eating, you can break or cut each patty into two or three bite-size pieces). Dunk in the sauce and eat.

/ CONTINUED

NOTES /

To speed up prep, chop the peanuts and green onions in a small food processor.

Boil the noodles and ready the lettuce, herbs, and sauce in advance and refrigerate separately. To refresh the noodles, sprinkle with water and microwave on high for 60 to 90 seconds.

For extra color and texture, cut a 2-inch section of carrot into fine matchsticks (or coarsely grate it), then add to the dipping sauce. The beef is also great in rice noodle salad bowls (see page 197).

For **curry-scented grilled beef rice bowls**, cut the lettuce into ribbons, coarsely chop the herbs, and put them in soup bowls. Add room temperature or slightly warm cooked rice (about ¾ cup per bowl) and the cooked beef, then drizzle with the sauce. Eat with a fork and spoon.

BE SKEPTICAL ABOUT THE COOKING INSTRUCTIONS ON YOUR NOODLE PACKAGE

Japanese and a handful of Chinese noodle companies have spot-on cooking directions, but most producers don't. Plus, the noodles are crafted for multiple uses. Go rogue and judge the timing and doneness yourself. You'll be a better cook.

BEEF STEW with star anise and lemongrass

SERVES 4 TO 6

TAKES ABOUT 1¼ HOURS

2 pounds trimmed boneless
beef chuck, cut into
1½-inch chunks

1½ teaspoons Chinese
five-spice powder

2 teaspoons packed light or
dark brown sugar

3 tablespoons fish sauce,
plus more as needed

2 to 3 tablespoons canola or
other neutral oil

2 large garlic cloves,
finely chopped

3 tablespoons finely chopped
peeled ginger

1 cup chopped shallot or
yellow onion

1½ cups canned crushed
tomatoes in puree, or
2 cups chopped peeled
tomatoes

2 large or 3 medium stalks
lemongrass, trimmed, cut
into 3-inch lengths, and
bruised with a meat mallet
or heavy saucepan

1 bay leaf

2 whole star anise
(16 robust points total)

Fine sea salt

2 to 2½ cups water

1 pound carrots, peeled and
cut into 1-inch chunks

¼ cup coarsely chopped
fresh cilantro, mint, or basil

Typically enjoyed with a baguette, *bò kho* is an iconic Viet-Franco dish. The traditional version requires a lengthy simmer, which has deterred me from making it more often. But I discovered that a pressure cooker shortens the cooking time to a good hour, and the traditional marinating period isn't needed. Suddenly, the Vietnamese classic became doable for a weeknight.

Bread and *bò kho* are great friends, but you can also serve the stew over boiled egg or rice noodles (select pappardelle-size noodles, such as A Taste of Thai brand). Add a green salad for a complete meal. This stew develops fabulous flavor when made one or two days ahead. Store, covered, in the refrigerator.

/

In a large bowl, combine the beef, five-spice powder, brown sugar, and fish sauce and stir to coat. Set aside.

Warm a 6-quart pressure cooker over high heat until very hot. Add 2 to 3 teaspoons of the canola oil and then, in three batches, sear the beef on all sides, 2 to 3 minutes total (don't expect deep browning since the meat is wettish); transfer the seared beef to a plate. Add oil between batches as needed; and as you sear, reserve any leftover marinade in its bowl. (To sear the beef in a multicooker, choose a high heat setting, such as Brown on the Fagor Lux, or adjust the Sauté function on the Instant Pot.)

Turn the heat to medium-low, then add the garlic, ginger, and shallot. Continue cooking, stirring, for 3 to 4 minutes, until no longer raw smelling. Add the tomatoes, lemongrass, bay leaf, star anise, and ½ teaspoon salt, then turn the heat to high. Let simmer and bubble for 4 to 6 minutes, until the mixture resembles a rough wet paste, stirring occasionally to prevent sticking. (If using a multicooker, lower the heat setting to cook the aromatics, then raise it again for the tomato and other ingredients. Between heat adjustments, you may have to turn off the machine.)

Return the beef, its juice, and any reserved marinade to the cooker, give them a big stir, and add enough of the water to cover the beef.

/ CONTINUED

Lock the lid in place. Bring to high pressure, adjust the heat to maintain pressure, and cook for 10 minutes. Then, remove from the heat, depressurize naturally for 15 minutes, and release the residual pressure. (If using a multicooker, add enough water to *barely* cover the meat, program the machine to cook at high pressure for 10 minutes, turn it off or unplug it, and depressurize for 18 minutes before releasing residual pressure.)

Unlock the cooker. The beef should be chewy-tender; when you press on a chunk, it should yield but still feel firm. Skim off the fat, if needed, and add the carrots. Return to a swift simmer and cook, uncovered, for about 30 minutes, until the beef and vegetables are both tender and the sauce flavors have intensified. (On a multicooker, choose a medium- or low-heat setting, such as Sauté or Simmer on the Fagor Lux, or adjust the Sauté function on the Instant Pot.) Let the stew rest, uncovered, for 5 to 10 minutes. Taste and, if needed, add more salt or fish sauce to intensify the flavor, or splash in water to lighten it. Divide the stew among shallow bowls, removing and discarding the lemongrass, bay leaf, and star anise, and garnish with the cilantro. Serve warm.

NOTES /

To finely chop the garlic, ginger, and onion in a food processor, coarsely chop each one and then pulse together.

Crushed tomatoes are usually available in 28-ounce cans, which contain about 3½ cups. No use for the leftovers? Start from a 28-ounce can of whole peeled tomatoes: strain and save the juices for Bloody Marys, pulse the tomatoes in a food processor, and measure out the 2 cups needed for the recipe.

Can't find fresh lemongrass? Substitute ¼ cup lemongrass paste.

To prepare the stew without a pressure cooker, season and then marinate the beef for 30 minutes. Use a 5-quart Dutch oven to sear the beef and cook the stew as directed, but increase the water to 3½ cups and simmer, covered, for 1¼ hours. Uncover, add the carrots, and finish cooking.

6

In Vietnam, meat is precious and
Buddhist traditions are strong,
so it isn't surprising that eggs and
soybeans are important in everyone's
diet. This chapter offers easy and
satisfying low-meat and no-meat
dishes. Look for vegetarian options
in other chapters too!

EGGS, TOFU,
and tempeh

HERBY OVEN-STEAMED *eggs*

SERVES 4 TO 6

TAKES ABOUT 1 HOUR

1½ ounces dried glass
noodles (saifun or bean
thread noodles; see
page 14)

6 ounces ground pork (about
85% lean) or ground turkey
thigh or chicken thigh

⅓ cup finely chopped shallot
or yellow onion

¼ cup lightly packed
chopped fresh cilantro,
basil, or parsley

2 tablespoons fish sauce

1 tablespoon canola or other
neutral oil

½ teaspoon plus ⅛ teaspoon
recently ground black pepper

Rounded ½ teaspoon sugar

½ cup plus 1 tablespoon
water

5 eggs

Chile garlic sauce (see
page 31), sriracha, or
sambal oelek (optional,
for heat seekers)

Sometimes translated as "Vietnamese meat loaf," this dish is Viet comfort food—pork, shallot, seasonings, and plump glass noodles, suspended in eggy goodness. People enjoy *trứng hấp* (steamed eggs) as a main or side dish, at home as well as at restaurants—especially ones selling broken rice plates. It's humble, popular fare.

The egg mixture is traditionally cooked in a Chinese steamer, but for this book, I wanted a cooking alternative to the traditional method. After experimenting for two weeks, I settled on baking the dish in a hot water bath. The egg mixture actually tasted richer and looked more elegant than the humble original, with a creamy layer on top. Serve with rice or another grain, pair with a salad for a light meal, or spread atop crackers, bread, or cucumber slices. Pictured here with the main recipe is a meatless, mushroomy variation in the Notes.

/

In a mixing bowl or 4-cup measuring cup, soak the noodles in hot water for 5 to 10 minutes, until pliable.

Meanwhile, preheat the oven to 325°F. Bring a kettle of water to a boil, turning the heat to low to keep it hot, if needed. Select a baking dish about 2 inches deep and large enough to hold four 8-ounce ramekins, about 4 inches in diameter; or six 5½-ounce ramekins, about 3½ inches in diameter. A dish with handles makes transporting easier.

Drain the noodles and then chop into short rods, no longer than ¾ inch, and return them to the mixing bowl. Add the pork, shallot, cilantro, fish sauce, canola oil, pepper, and sugar and use a fork to vigorously mash, stir, and fold to break up the meat and mix well. Add the ½ cup plus 1 tablespoon water, stirring until incorporated, then add the eggs, stirring and beating to thoroughly mix.

Stir the egg mixture again and divide among the ramekins. Transfer the ramekins to the baking dish and pour in enough hot water to come halfway up the sides of the ramekins. Cover the baking dish with aluminum foil and slide into the oven.

/ CONTINUED

Bake for 35 to 40 minutes, then check the progress; the tops should be domed, look opaque, and feel firm to the touch. When you insert a toothpick, a little liquid should emerge. If needed, bake 5 minutes longer and recheck. The baking time will depend on the baking dish material and the size of the ramekins.

Remove from the oven and let the ramekins rest in the baking dish for 5 minutes, loosely covered by the foil. Then, using tongs or oven mitts, carefully remove the ramekins. When cooling, the buttercup-colored tops will turn a less pretty light beige, but the good flavor will remain.

Serve the eggs hot, warm, or at room temperature, with the chile sauce, if you like.

NOTES /

Leftovers will keep, covered, in the refrigerator for up to 3 days. To reheat, microwave the individual ramekins for 20 to 30 seconds.

For **mushroomy oven-steamed eggs**, omit the meat and substitute 8 ounces chopped cremini or white mushrooms (include caps and stems, and chop by hand or in the food processor; aim for pinkie-nail-wide pieces). Cook the mushrooms in a large skillet over medium-high heat with 1 tablespoon canola oil and season with several big pinches of salt. When they're half their original volume, after 2 to 3 minutes, remove from the heat and let rest for 5 minutes. Mix the mushrooms with the noodles, shallot, oil, pepper, and sugar. Add 3 tablespoons chopped cilantro, 1½ tablespoons fish sauce (or 1 tablespoon soy sauce plus a rounded ½ teaspoon fine sea salt), the water, and 6 eggs. Bake as directed.

SHAKING tofu

SERVES 2 OR 3

TAKES 30 MINUTES

TOFU

14 to 16 ounces extra-firm
tofu (see page 23)

Rounded ¼ teaspoon fine
sea salt, plus ⅛ teaspoon

1 large clove garlic, put
through a press or minced
and mashed

1 tablespoon sugar

½ teaspoon cornstarch

½ teaspoon recently ground
black pepper

1½ tablespoons Bragg Liquid
Aminos, Maggi Seasoning
sauce, or soy sauce

1 teaspoon toasted sesame oil

3 tablespoons water

1 tablespoon neutral oil

SALAD

¼ cup thinly sliced red onion
or shallot

1½ teaspoons sugar or honey

2 pinches fine sea salt

About 4 grinds black pepper

1½ tablespoons unseasoned
rice vinegar

2 tablespoons water

4 cups lightly packed
watercress, arugula,
or baby lettuce mix

¼ cup fresh mint, basil, or
other herb leaves, torn

8 cherry tomatoes (optional)

I love shaking beef (see page 136), but when I want a meatless dish, I opt for this version. Cubes of tofu are first pan-seared, to enrich and build umami character, and then cooked in a peppery, salty-sweet sauce and presented atop lightly dressed salad greens. Bragg Liquid Aminos or Maggi Seasoning sauce lends a meaty flavor, but the color will be richer if you use soy sauce.

Lightly salting the tofu helps it brown beautifully. Fry the tofu up to 4 hours in advance and set aside, covered, at room temperature. Close to serving time, prep the salad and then warm the tofu in a skillet over medium heat until gently sizzling. Add the seasoning sauce and continue as directed.

/

To prepare the tofu Cut the tofu into 1-inch cubes and season with the rounded ¼ teaspoon salt, then let drain on a double layer of paper towels or a clean, non-terry dish towel for 10 to 15 minutes.

Meanwhile, in a small bowl, combine the garlic, sugar, cornstarch, remaining ⅛ teaspoon salt, pepper, Bragg Liquid Aminos, sesame oil, and water and stir to mix. Set the sauce aside with the oil.

To make the salad Rinse the onion in a strainer under cold running water for about 10 seconds; set aside. In a large bowl (suitable for tossing the salad), whisk together the sugar, salt, pepper, vinegar, and water. Add the onion and top with the watercress and mint; if using the tomatoes, halve each and add to the bowl. Do *not* toss.

In a large nonstick or carbon-steel skillet over medium-high heat, warm the oil. Meanwhile, use paper towel to blot excess moisture from the tofu.

When the oil shimmers, add the tofu and cook for 5 to 6 minutes, turning frequently to brown on two or three sides. Turn the heat to medium, pour in the seasoning sauce, and cook for 2 to 4 minutes, until the sauce reduces and clings to the tofu. Remove from the heat.

Quickly toss the salad and transfer everything, dressing included, to a platter or serving dish. Crown with the tofu and any lingering sauce in the pan. At the table, combine the ingredients and dive in.

SRIRACHA tofu

SERVES 4

TAKES 20 MINUTES

10 ounces super-firm tofu
   (see page 23)

1 tablespoon water

1 tablespoon Bragg Liquid
   Aminos or Maggi Seasoning
   sauce

2½ to 3 tablespoons
   sriracha (use the maximum
   for a nice lick of heat)

1 tablespoon canola or other
   neutral oil

I grew up with tofu, but for people who are new to it, cooking with tofu can be challenging. What if it falls apart? What if it's bland? Don't worry, because tofu is forgiving. It takes on big flavors super-well, so season with abandon!

Sturdy and bold, this simple tofu is fantastic for rice paper rolls, sandwiches, salads, fried rice, stir-fries, and soup toppings (see the porridge embellishments on page 73). It's like baked tofu but prepared in a skillet. Thin pieces of super-firm tofu are cooked until coated all over with a spicy-salty match that is made in heaven: sriracha and Bragg Liquid Aminos. Then, the tofu is gently fried to lock in the flavors. To sub extra-firm tofu, see the Notes.

/

Cut the tofu crosswise into three thick slabs, each a scant 1 inch thick. Then, cut each slab crosswise into eight strips, each roughly ¼ inch thick and 2 inches long. The strips will resemble dominoes. (It's easy to cut relatively even strips if you repeatedly halve the tofu pieces.)

In a large nonstick skillet, combine the water, Bragg Liquid Aminos, and sriracha and stir to mix. Add the tofu and turn several times, then arrange flat in the skillet for maximum exposure to the seasonings. Set the skillet over medium heat and when bubbling begins, about 2 minutes, use chopsticks or a silicone spatula to flip the tofu. Continue cooking to allow the seasonings to concentrate and stick to the tofu. When little liquid remains in the pan, about 2 minutes, drizzle 1½ teaspoons of the canola oil over the tofu. Shake the pan to dislodge the tofu and flip the pieces again.

Let the tofu gently sizzle for 3 to 4 minutes to dry out and brown. Midway through cooking, when the underside is mottled orange or maybe browned, drizzle on the remaining 1½ teaspoons canola oil and flip the tofu. The finished tofu will have an orange-brown color with some dark brown spots.

Remove the pan from the heat and let the sizzling subside, then transfer the tofu to a rack. Let the tofu rest for 5 to 10 minutes to cool and dry before using. The tofu can be stored in an airtight container in the refrigerator for up to 5 days (freezing dries out the tofu slightly).

NOTES /

When used as a component in other dishes, note that this recipe yields 10 ounces.

If super-firm tofu is unavailable or you want tender-firm results, use a 14- to 16-ounce tub of extra-firm tofu. If the tofu came as a two-pack, halve each block crosswise and then cut each of the smaller blocks into three square-ish slabs, about ½ inch thick. If there's a single block, quarter it and then cut each small block crosswise into three slabs. Regardless, you'll have twelve pieces total.

Because extra-firm tofu releases more water than super-firm tofu, omit the 1 tablespoon water. Proceed as directed, but flip the tofu more often to make sure the seasonings stick and coat without burning up. Add the oil after things look dry-ish, and raise the heat slightly to gently fry for 4 to 5 minutes to enrich and seal in the seasonings. Yields 12 ounces.

To make **char siu tofu**, replace the Bragg Liquid Aminos and sriracha with ¼ teaspoon Chinese five-spice powder, 1 tablespoon hoisin sauce, 1 tablespoon soy sauce, and 1 tablespoon maple syrup. Cut and cook the super-firm or extra-firm tofu as directed.

SPICY SWEET POMEGRANATE tofu

SERVES 4

TAKES 35 MINUTES

14 to 16 ounces extra-firm
tofu (see page 23)

About ¾ teaspoon fine
sea salt

3½ tablespoons water

2 tablespoons pomegranate
molasses (see page 34)

1½ tablespoons soy sauce

1 tablespoon sriracha,
plus more as needed

1½ teaspoons to
1½ tablespoons light or
dark brown sugar

¾ teaspoon cornstarch

2½ tablespoons canola or
other neutral oil

6 large cremini or white
mushrooms, quartered,
with stems intact

¼ cup finely chopped shallot
or yellow onion

2 garlic cloves, finely chopped

2 Anaheim, Hatch, or sweet
red chiles, trimmed and cut
into 1-inch squares

This earthy, tangy main dish shares a sauce similar to the
Pomegranate Sriracha Shrimp on page 109, but the tofu, soy sauce,
and vegetables turn it into something distinctively delicious. Tofu
is typically deep-fried for dishes like this one, but panfrying is
a healthier way to inject richness and character. The technique
used here is the same as for Shaking Tofu on page 149. For texture,
complexity, and color, I add mushroom and mild-tasting chiles.
Anaheims are my go-to but during the warmer months when chiles
are in season, I love to use varieties such as Hatch and Corno di Toro.
In a major pinch, half a large bell pepper will do.

/

Cut the tofu into 1-inch cubes and season with a rounded ¼ teaspoon
of the salt, then let drain on a double layer of paper towels or a clean
non-terry dish towel for 10 to 15 minutes.

Meanwhile, in a small bowl, combine the remaining ½ teaspoon salt,
3 tablespoons of the water, the pomegranate molasses, soy sauce, and
sriracha. Taste and add the brown sugar, starting with 1½ teaspoons,
to create a tart sweetness; the amount you use will depend on the
flavor of the molasses and your own palate. For more heat, add more
sriracha, ½ teaspoon at a time. Aim for a tangy-savory-spicy dance
of flavors. Set the sauce aside. In another small bowl, stir together
the cornstarch and remaining 1½ teaspoons water and set aside.

In a large nonstick or carbon-steel skillet over medium-high or high
heat, warm 1 tablespoon of the canola oil. Meanwhile, use paper
towel to blot excess moisture from the tofu.

When the oil shimmers, add the tofu and cook for 5 to 6 minutes,
turning frequently to brown on two or three sides. Remove from
the pan and set aside on a plate.

Add the mushrooms to the hot skillet and cook for 2 minutes,
until slightly shrunken, a bit browned, and glistening. Swirl in the
remaining 1½ tablespoons canola oil, add the shallot and garlic,
and stir-fry for about 30 seconds, until fragrant. Add the chiles

/ CONTINUED

and stir-fry for about 1 minute, until slightly softened. Return the tofu to the pan and cook for about 2 minutes, until hot.

Stir the sauce and add to the pan, combining it with the vegetables. Cook at a vigorous boil for 1 minute, stirring, until slightly thickened. Give the cornstarch slurry a stir, pour into the pan, and cook, stirring, for 20 to 30 seconds to thicken the sauce and coat the tofu and vegetables.

Transfer everything to a plate or shallow bowl and serve.

NOTES /

There's some sputtering with this dish. Put newspaper on the floor next to the stove to make cleanup easier.

Instead of pomegranate molasses, use tamarind liquid, concentrate, or paste. For guidance and substitution ratios, see page 35.

The tofu can be panfried 4 hours in advance and kept, covered, at room temperature.

LEMONGRASS tempeh crumbles

SERVES 4

TAKES 25 MINUTES

½ cup coarsely chopped
lemongrass (from 2 large
stalks)

1½ tablespoons coarsely
chopped garlic

¼ cup coarsely chopped
shallot

Rounded 1 tablespoon sugar

1 tablespoon sriracha,
plus more for serving

2 tablespoons Bragg Liquid
Aminos, Maggi Seasoning
sauce, or soy sauce

¼ cup water

Brimming 3 tablespoons
canola or other neutral oil

8 ounces tempeh, broken
into thumbnail-size chunks

1 teaspoon raw or toasted
sesame seeds (optional)

2 green onions, green part
only, cut into rings

Fine sea salt

1 small English or 2 Persian
cucumbers, thinly sliced
(optional)

When my husband saw this on the counter, he mistook it for the caramelized porky crumbles on page 132. Yes, they look alike, but these crumbles are vegan, with a citrusy and spicy edge. Tempeh isn't a Viet ingredient, but I've used it in banh mi, pho, and here to mimic meat. When crumbled into small pieces in this recipe, tempeh absorbs the seasonings well and fries up nicely. Whether made from meat or tempeh, these sorts of crumbles are used the same way—to mix into and season rice, kind of like a condiment. Add a side of radish and carrot pickle (see page 29) for refreshing crunch and tang. The crumbles will keep, covered, in the refrigerator, for up to 3 days (though they never last long in my house) and are good scooped up with tortilla chips.

/

In a small food processor, whirl the lemongrass to finely chop. Add the garlic and shallot and process until everything is minced, pausing to scrape down the sides as needed; set aside. (If you don't have a small food processor, grate the lemongrass stalks and mince the garlic and shallot.) In a small bowl, mix together the sugar, sriracha, Bragg Liquid Aminos, and water. Set the seasoning liquid aside.

In a large skillet over medium heat, warm the canola oil. Add the lemongrass mixture and cook, stirring, for about 1 minute, until fragrant and no longer raw smelling. Add the tempeh and seasoning liquid, turn the heat to medium-high, and let the mixture bubble and fry for about 10 minutes. At first, press on the tempeh to break it into smaller pieces (ideally, separate into individual soybeans) to maximize flavor and crisping. When satisfied, leave the tempeh to sizzle, giving it an occasional stir and then spreading it out to cover the bottom of the pan so it cooks evenly.

Toward the end of the 10 minutes, when some of the tempeh is golden brown, add the sesame seeds (if using) and cook, stirring frequently, for about 2 minutes longer to brown the tempeh further. The mixture will feel lighter under the weight of your spatula. When most of the tempeh is golden brown, remove from the heat,

/ CONTINUED

stir in the green onions, and let rest for 5 minutes to deepen in flavor. Taste and, if needed, add salt, a pinch at a time.

Serve the tempeh warm or at room temperature, with the cucumber, if desired. If diners want more heat, pass additional sriracha.

NOTE /

For the best flavor, use old-school all-soybean tempeh, such as Westsoy and Lifelight brands, available at many health food markets; tempeh made with grains lack the umami depth of the traditional kind. When fresh lemongrass is unavailable, substitute 3 to 4 tablespoons lemongrass paste.

LEMONGRASS PREP TIPS AND SHORTCUTS

When dealing with lemongrass, remember this: You can't chew what you can't chop. To trim a stalk, chop off the green, woody top section and the tough base. Remove loose or dry outer layers. The usable section will be 4 to 8 inches long, depending on the stalk size.

To chop a trimmed stalk, cut it into 4-inch sections, halve each lengthwise, cut crosswise into half circles, then chop to the desired texture. If you like, whack the stalk with a meat mallet or heavy saucepan to break up the fibers before cutting.

Reduce knife work by grating the stalk with a rasp grater such as a Microplane; chop pieces that eventually splay open. Use 1½ tablespoons grated lemongrass for every 2 tablespoons chopped lemongrass. Feel free to apply this 3:4 ratio when subbing frozen minced lemongrass (see below) or store-bought lemongrass paste for freshly chopped lemongrass.

For advance prep, freeze trimmed stalks in a zipper-top bag for up to 3 months. Or, chop the stalks into ¼-inch pieces and then blitz in a processor, 1 cup at a time, to a fine mincelike texture. Add 1 tablespoon neutral oil and pulse to combine. Freeze in a storage container for up to 3 months.

SHIITAKE AND TOFU frittata

SERVES 2

TAKES 30 MINUTES

3 dried shiitake mushrooms

7 to 8 ounces firm tofu
(see page 23)

⅓ cup chopped green onion,
white and green parts

¼ teaspoon fine sea salt

Rounded ⅛ teaspoon recently
ground black pepper

1½ teaspoons Bragg Liquid
Aminos, Maggi Seasoning
sauce, or soy sauce

3 eggs

About 1 tablespoon canola or
other neutral oil

2 to 3 teaspoons chile garlic
sauce (see page 31) or
sambal oelek (optional)

1 tablespoon soy sauce
(optional)

When I want a tasty blast from my childhood, I whip up one of these little frittatas—essentially an open-faced, flat omelet. Called *chả trứng chiên* in Vietnamese, it's great with rice or even slid into a banh mi (see page 62). I grew up eating the classic version with ground pork, but nowadays I often make a tofu rendition. If you can't decide between them, make both (see the Notes for the meaty version). The recipe makes one frittata, but you can always tinker and do a side-by-side taste test of vegetarian versus one made with ground pork, turkey, or chicken. Leftovers keep well for up to 3 days.

/

In a medium bowl, combine the mushrooms and ½ cup hot water and let hydrate for about 15 minutes, until the mushrooms are plump and soft. Meanwhile, break the tofu into four or five chunks, wrap in muslin or a non-terry dish towel, and squeeze and massage over the sink to expel liquid, crushing the tofu at the same time. Transfer to a medium bowl.

Strain the rehydrated mushrooms, reserving 1 tablespoon of the liquid. Gently squeeze the mushrooms to expel excess moisture, then trim off the stems, chop the caps into pea-size pieces, and add to the tofu along with the green onion, salt, pepper, and Bragg Liquid Aminos, using a fork to combine well. Add the eggs, then stir and fold to incorporate into a thick mixture.

In a small nonstick skillet (or a well-seasoned carbon-steel or cast-iron one) over medium-low heat, warm 2 teaspoons of the canola oil. When the oil is hot and nearly shimmering, stir the egg mixture and pour into the skillet, spreading it out into a flat layer. After about 3 minutes, when it's bubbling around the edge, cover the pan and cook for about 5 minutes, until the top is opaque yellow but still wet in the middle.

Uncover the skillet and fry for 3 to 4 minutes longer, until the frittata's underside is golden brown and the top is firm enough for you to turn without splattering. If the top is wet and jiggly, re-cover and cook for 30 seconds before rechecking. Holding the skillet handle with one hand, use your other hand to slide a spatula under the frittata, lift it, and then confidently flip it over.

For a touch of luxe, dribble the remaining 1 teaspoon oil around the edge and continue gently frying for 2 to 3 minutes, until browned on the second side.

Transfer the frittata to a plate and cut into wedges. Serve, hot, warm, or at room temperature. Eat with a dab of chile sauce or mix the soy sauce and reserved 1 tablespoon mushroom-soaking liquid for dunking. Or, eat with both.

NOTES /

For a meatier flavor, season the frittata with Bragg Liquid Aminos. For dipping, I prefer soy sauce or chile sauce.

For a **shiitake and meat frittata**, use 6 ounces ground pork, turkey thigh, or chicken thigh instead of the tofu. Omit the Bragg Liquid Aminos, add the green onions, and season with ½ teaspoon plus ⅛ teaspoon fine sea salt and the black pepper. If you use ground chicken, cook a little longer while the frittata pan is covered, because it's more moist than other ground meats.

7

Traditional Vietnamese salads are tasty but too complicated for weeknight meals. Given that, the salads in this chapter were streamlined to be more doable but still thrilling. Ditto for the cooked vegetable sides, which are similarly modern but rooted in good Viet cooking.

SALADS AND
vegetable sides

GREEN MANGO, CABBAGE, AND jicama salad

SERVES 4 TO 6

TAKES 40 MINUTES

2 cups packed thinly sliced
green cabbage

½ small jicama, peeled and
cut into medium-thick
matchsticks

One 16-ounce unripe mango,
peeled, pitted, and cut into
thick matchsticks (double
the width of the jicama)

1 lime

Unseasoned rice vinegar
as needed

1½ to 2 tablespoons sugar

1½ to 2 tablespoons fish
sauce, or 1½ tablespoons
soy sauce plus ¼ teaspoon
fine sea salt

1 small garlic clove, put
through a press or minced
and mashed

1 Thai or small serrano chile,
finely chopped, with
seeds intact

¼ cup packed coarsely
chopped fresh mint or basil

⅓ cup finely chopped
unsalted roasted peanuts
or cashews

Many people assume that an unripe mango is not ready for prime time, but to me, it's an opportunity to make *gỏi xoài* (mango salad). The traditional rendition includes cooked shrimp and fatty pork, but I've found that dropping the proteins not only makes the salad less fussy (read: faster to make) but also shifts the focus to the produce and highlights the tropical flavor combinations that are central to Vietnamese cooking. The decluttered version is lighter, brighter, and easily adapted for vegan diners.

At the store, choose a rock-hard, unripe mango (one with all or mostly green skin). Store it in the fridge to prevent ripening. When you're ready to make the salad, peel it with a knife or vegetable peeler, removing all vestiges of the firm green skin. The remaining flesh sweetens slightly and softens in the salad. For the jicama, choose a small, blemish-free one (ideally no larger than a grapefruit); it will be sweeter and less starchy than older, bigger ones.

/

In a large bowl, combine the cabbage, jicama, and mango and set aside. (The vegetables and fruit can be stored, covered, in the refrigerator for up to 24 hours.)

Using a fine rasp grater, such as a Microplane, zest the lime directly into a small bowl. Squeeze the lime to get 2 tablespoons of juice; if you're short, add vinegar to make up the difference. Add the lime juice to the zest and then add 1½ tablespoons sugar. Stir to dissolve the sugar, then taste and add more sugar, if needed, for a strong tart-sweet finish. Add enough of the fish sauce to arrive at a bold, salty-tangy finish. Add the garlic and chile, stir, and then set the dressing aside.

Toss the vegetables and fruit well with the dressing, mint, and peanuts, until the cabbage and jicama soften slightly. Transfer to a shallow serving bowl, leaving excess dressing behind.

Serve immediately.

/ CONTINUED

NOTES /

Sometimes sold in the produce section, jicama snack sticks, which are the size of steak fries, can be cut smaller and used for this salad. You need only 1 cup of jicama matchsticks.

For extra protein flair, add 4 ounces cooked shrimp or sliced Sriracha Tofu (page 150).

When mango is unavailable, make a **peach, cabbage, and jicama salad**. Substitute 2 medium-firm, unripe peaches for the mango. Keep the fuzz on, if you are not allergic to it. Expect to produce irregular peach matchsticks because of the fruit's natural contours. Just aim for sticklike pieces that will mix well with the other veggies.

MASTERING MATCHSTICKS

When an ingredient is cut into matchsticks, its color, flavor, and texture are preserved as it commingles with the other components of a dish. Size-wise, matchsticks are about 3 inches long. A regular (medium) one is roughly ⅛ inch thick, the width of a fat bean sprout (cut them skinnier for thin matchsticks). Medium-large ones are a little bigger, like two skinny bean sprouts. For a thick matchstick, think a good ¼ inch, the broad end of a chopstick.

When cutting a daikon or similar vegetable, cut it crosswise into shorter sections, and then cut a thin cheek off each one, so it sits flat on a cutting board. You'll be able to make even slices, which can be stacked and cut into matchsticks. Quarter a jicama so each section sits flat for safe slicing and cutting.

When working with a skinny carrot, cut it diagonally into thin slices; the angle of your knife will determine the length of the sticks. Arrange the slices into several short stacks and cut into slender pieces, curling your fingertips under for safety. The matchsticks won't be uniform in length, but there's beauty in imperfection. Your Viet dishes will sparkle with character.

SMACKED CUCUMBER AND shrimp salad

SERVES 4

TAKES 15 MINUTES

1 medium English cucumber

¼ teaspoon fine sea salt

¼ teaspoon sugar, plus
   1 tablespoon

1 tablespoon fresh lime juice

2½ teaspoons fish sauce

½ Fresno or jalapeño
   chile, finely chopped, or
   2 teaspoons chile garlic
   sauce (see page 31)

2 tablespoons chopped
   unsalted roasted peanuts
   or cashews (optional, but
   great for richness)

¾ cup small cooked shrimp
   or shredded cooked
   chicken (optional)

Want a fast Vietnamese-style salad? Make this one. It's my simplified version of *gỏi dưa leo*, a combination of thinly sliced cucumber, carrot, peanuts, and shrimp, plus chicken or pork. The traditional version of that *gỏi*, the generic term for Viet celebration salads, requires a generous time commitment. My work-around borrows the Chinese technique of smacking the cucumber to slightly crush its flesh and expose it to flavor fast. It's a terrific time-saver. Chilling the cucumber is key to obtaining bright flavor.

Instead of English cucumber, substitute 12 ounces of Persian, Japanese, or another kind of thin-skinned cucumber. They're skinnier, so cut them in half lengthwise and then on the diagonal.

/

Trim the ends off the cucumber. Using a heavy cleaver or the bottom of a saucepan, smack the cucumber from one end to the other; it will crack and open up. Using a knife, separate and cut it lengthwise into four long pieces; the smacking has done some of that for you already, so let it naturally guide you. Angle your knife to cut each cucumber section into dramatically thick slices, each roughly ¼ inch thick; they won't all look the same. Put into a bowl and toss with the salt and ¼ teaspoon sugar. Refrigerate, uncovered, for at least 10 minutes, or up to 1 hour, while the cucumber releases liquid.

Meanwhile, in a small bowl, stir together the remaining 1 tablespoon sugar, the lime juice, fish sauce, and chile to make a dressing.

Drain the cucumber in a mesh strainer, shake out excess liquid, and transfer to a large bowl. Add the dressing, and peanuts and shrimp, if desired. Taste and adjust the flavors as needed.

Pile the salad into a shallow bowl and serve immediately.

SPICY BROCCOLI AND *herb slaw*

SERVES 4

TAKES 20 MINUTES

One 12-ounce package
  broccoli slaw

1½ tablespoons sugar

3 tablespoons fresh lime juice

1½ tablespoons fish sauce

1 very small garlic clove, put
  through a press or minced
  and mashed

1 Thai or small serrano
  chile, finely chopped, with
  seeds intact

4 ounces shredded cooked
  chicken, or 10 pieces
  Sriracha Tofu (page 150),
  cut into narrow strips

⅓ cup coarsely chopped
  fresh cilantro, mint, or basil

Mild-tasting, crunchy fruits and vegetables, such as unripe green papaya and kohlrabi, are often featured in popular Vietnamese salads. They're cut into matchsticks and tossed with a protein of some sort, lots of fresh herbs, and a tangy dressing. Such salads dazzle with color, textures, and flavor.

As I wandered my local Safeway's produce section, looking for worthy substitutes, I came upon bags of broccoli coleslaw, which is resourcefully made from the plant's stems. Pale green and interspersed with carrot pieces, the slaw was a time-saving bonus—no peeling, chopping, or slicing! Most Americans substitute packaged broccoli slaw for cabbage in mayonnaise-based slaws, but I had a healthful Viet salad in mind.

My husband was skeptical of the woody broccoli pieces. I changed his mind after I blanched the slaw in hot water to soften it slightly, which made it turn jadelike, and also made it more receptive to the dressing. This modern salad comes together in a jiffy and tastes special, despite its humble beginnings. That's very Vietnamese.

/

Put the slaw in a medium heatproof bowl and pour freshly boiled water over it to cover. In about 30 seconds, the slaw should have softened enough for you to easily bend a piece of broccoli so the ends touch. Drain in a colander, rinse with water, and set aside to cool and drain well.

In a small bowl, combine the sugar, lime juice, and fish sauce, stirring to dissolve the sugar. Taste to make sure it has a balanced tart-sweet-salty flavor. Stir in the garlic and chile, then set the dressing aside.

Transfer the drained slaw to a large bowl. Add the chicken, cilantro, and dressing and toss well, then let sit for 1 to 2 minutes to develop flavor and toss again.

Transfer the slaw to a serving plate, leaving most of the excess dressing behind. Serve immediately.

ZESTY LIME-CHILE vinaigrette

MAKES ½ CUP; ENOUGH TO DRESS 2 SALADS

TAKES 15 MINUTES

2 limes (smooth-skinned ones are juicier)

Unseasoned rice vinegar as needed

1½ tablespoons sugar or honey

1½ tablespoons soy sauce

1½ tablespoons canola or other neutral oil

Fine sea salt

Recently ground black pepper

½ large jalapeño or Fresno chile, seeded and finely chopped

Vietnamese salads get their inspiration from both East and West. There are tropical salads dressed with fish sauce, lime, and chile (see pages 163 to 166), but also European-style salads dressed with tangy, slightly rich vinaigrettes too. This dressing straddles many cultures. I originally conceived it for a slaw, but over time, I realized that the lime zest–laden dressing was more than a one-trick wonder. Its zippy, fresh flavor is great for a wide range of salads.

Make a batch and use it for one of the subrecipes on the next page; each salad serves 4, but they are easily doubled to satisfy vegetable fiends or to serve more people.

/

Using a fine-rasp grater, such as a Microplane, zest the limes directly into a small bowl. Squeeze the limes to get ¼ cup of juice; if you're short, add vinegar to make up the difference. Add the lime juice to the zest and then add the sugar, soy sauce, and canola oil. Stir to dissolve the sugar, then taste and season with salt and pepper to create a balanced, savory-tangy note (I usually begin with ¼ teaspoon salt and ⅛ teaspoon pepper).

When satisfied, add the chile and let sit for 5 to 10 minutes to develop more flavor before using. (Or, transfer to a lidded jar; the vinaigrette will keep in the refrigerator for up to 5 days. Beyond that, the acidic nature of the lime weakens a bit, but the vinaigrette is still great. Bring to room temperature before using.)

/ CONTINUED

simple green salad

Dress 5 to 6 cups of torn lettuce leaves (for lively texture, mix crisp romaine with soft-leaf lettuce, such as butter or Boston) with about ¼ cup of the vinaigrette.

quick slaw

Toss 4 cups of cabbage slaw with ¼ cup of the vinaigrette. If you like, dress it up with ¼ cup chopped fresh cilantro, mint, or basil. For texture, add a handful of chopped unsalted roasted peanuts or cashews.

watercress and herb salad

Use about ¼ cup vinaigrette to coat 3 cups watercress, 1 cup thinly sliced fennel (or carrot or radish), and 2 tablespoons chopped fresh cilantro, basil, or mint. If available, top with 2 tablespoons fried onions or shallots.

beet, carrot, and mint salad

Combine 1¼ cups coarsely grated or shredded raw beet with 1 cup coarsely grated or shredded raw carrot (use the largest hole of a box grater or the large shredder attachment of a food processor to prep the vegetables). Add ½ cup lightly packed hand-torn mint leaves, ¼ cup chopped unsalted roasted peanuts or cashews, and, if available, 2 to 3 tablespoons fried onions or shallots. Toss with ¼ cup vinaigrette and garnish with extra onions, if desired.

CHARRED BRUSSELS SPROUTS with coconut

SERVES 4

TAKES 15 MINUTES

1 pound small to medium
  brussels sprouts

2 tablespoons canola or
  other neutral oil

⅓ cup coconut water,
  plus more as needed

2 teaspoons fish sauce, or
  1 tablespoon soy sauce

The first time my family had brussels sprouts was in 1975 at the Camp Pendleton refugee resettlement facilities in Southern California. They were overcooked, sickly green, and gassy. We didn't eat them again until the early 2000s, when I served farm-fresh ones during the holiday season. My parents and siblings initially recoiled but changed their minds after the first bite. They liked and welcomed them to our table.

This dead-simple recipe is what I served for Thanksgiving in 2016. It's akin to oven-roasted brussels sprouts, but takes less time. The coconut water steam-cooks the sprouts and also lends sweetness to counter their slight bitterness. Fish sauce adds a lovely, low-key savory note, though you can substitute soy sauce. Don't have a pan large enough to cook the sprouts in one batch? Cook them in two batches in a medium skillet.

/

Trim a bit of the dry-ish stem end from each brussels sprout, discarding any leaves that fall off. Halve the sprouts from stem to top, transfer to a large bowl, and toss with 1 tablespoon of the canola oil. Set near the stove.

In a large skillet that holds heat well (such as cast iron, carbon steel, or stainless steel) over high heat, warm the remaining 1 tablespoon canola oil. Add the brussels sprouts, then use chopsticks or tongs to arrange them, cut-side down, in one layer and cook, without stirring, for 3 to 5 minutes, until well browned in spots on the cut side.

Lower the heat to medium, add the coconut water, and cover the pan with a lid or aluminum foil to steam for 3 to 4 minutes, until the liquid has evaporated. Uncover and poke one or two sprouts with the tip of a paring knife; they should be just tender. If they are not, add a splash or two of coconut water, which will help them cook a bit more via a shot of hot moisture.

Add the fish sauce, shake the pan and stir to distribute, and cook, uncovered, for about 1 minute longer to further develop the flavor and caramelize the brussels sprouts. If needed, raise the heat to coax the cooking. When the sprouts are lightly glazed, remove from the heat. Let rest for 1 minute.

Serve the sprouts hot, warm, or at room temperature.

NOTE /

To make a stunning-looking **charred cabbage with coconut**, cut 1¼ pounds of green cabbage (for easier cooking and handsome results, use a portion of a small head of cabbage) into 1-inch-thick wedges, keeping the core intact to hold the leaves together. Lightly spray oil on the cut sides (brushing or rubbing oil may make it too oily) and brown the wedges on their cut sides (there's no need to use extra oil during cooking). Add the coconut water and steam and finish as directed.

SPICY SHAVED brussels sprouts

SERVES 4

TAKES 15 MINUTES

2 or 3 garlic cloves, chopped
(use the maximum if you
like its boldness)

1 Fresno or jalapeño chile,
halved lengthwise and
thinly sliced crosswise,
with seeds intact

¼ teaspoon fine sea salt

2 tablespoons water

1 tablespoon unseasoned
rice vinegar

10 ounces brussels sprouts

1½ to 2 tablespoons canola
or other neutral oil (use
the maximum for extra
richness)

2 teaspoons soy sauce, or
1½ teaspoons fish sauce

Brussels sprouts have a wonderful bittersweet edge that can take on big flavors. Here, the seasoning mixture of garlic, chile, and diluted vinegar echo a garlic vinegar that's a popular condiment in Hanoi. After serving this mixture as a table condiment for pho, I began incorporating it into my repertoire to create a tangy-spicy-pungent undercurrent in sautés and stir-fries. The seasonings don't hit you over the head but rather unite and synergize all the ingredients.

/

In a small bowl, combine the garlic, chile, salt, water, and vinegar. Let the seasonings sit for 5 minutes (or even overnight) to develop flavor.

Meanwhile, trim a bit of the dry-ish stem end from each brussels sprout, discarding any leaves that fall off. Halve the sprouts from stem to top and, with the cut side facing down, cut each half into ⅛-inch-thick pieces. (If you like, use a food processor fitted with the slicing blade to thinly cut the sprouts.) Set near the stove.

In a large skillet over medium-high heat, warm the canola oil. When the oil is hot, add the sprouts and cook, stirring, for about 1 minute, until glistening and slightly softened. Lower the heat to medium, pour in the seasonings, and continue to cook, stirring, until crisp-tender, about 3 minutes. (Splash in a little water if things look dry.) Raise the heat to high, then pour in the soy sauce, stirring to combine, and cook for 15 to 30 seconds, until the sprouts absorb the liquid. Remove from the heat, transfer to a serving dish or shallow bowl, and serve hot or warm. They aren't bad at room temperature, either.

NOTE /

Brussels sprouts peak during the fall and winter, from October to February. Choose vivid green orbs that feel firm and heavy; smaller ones (about 1 inch in diameter) tend to taste sweeter, larger ones have a stronger cabbage-like quality. Cut the brussels sprouts by hand or in a food processor for texture and flavor that's better than packaged precut sprouts, which tend to be on the thicker side.

BLISTERED GREEN BEANS AND bacon

SERVES 4

TAKES 20 MINUTES

1 pound green beans,
   stem ends trimmed

Fine sea salt

⅛ teaspoon Chinese
   five-spice powder

2 teaspoons maple syrup,
   or 1 teaspoon honey plus
   1 teaspoon water

1½ teaspoons fish sauce

1 teaspoon soy sauce

1 teaspoon apple cider or
   distilled white vinegar

2 thick-cut slices smoked
   bacon, or 3 thin-cut
   slices smoked bacon,
   cut crosswise into ¼- to
   ⅓-inch-wide strips

2 garlic cloves, chopped

One of my favorite ways to stir-fry vegetables is to flavor them with Chinese sausage (*lạp cheung* in Cantonese; *lạp xưởng* in Vietnamese). The dry, sweet sausage isn't sold at regular supermarkets so I conjure up its flavors with smoky bacon, five-spice powder, and maple syrup.

Parboiling the green beans and then searing them in bacon fat ensures that they're cooked and full of deep savors. (The conventional Chinese method is to shallow fry them, but even I rarely want to heat up a wok filled with oil for that purpose.) If your stove has a booster burner for high heat, use it for this recipe.

/

Line a baking sheet with a clean dish towel or a double layer of paper towels.

Bring a large pot of salted water to a boil over high heat. Add the green beans and cook for 1 to 1½ minutes (there's no need to return to a boil), until they are a brilliant green and still crisp and snappy. Drain in a colander, then transfer to the prepared baking sheet and spread out to dry, finish cooking in their residual heat, and cool, about 10 minutes.

In a small bowl, stir together the five-spice powder, maple syrup, fish sauce, soy sauce, and vinegar. Set the seasoning liquid near the stove.

In a large skillet that holds heat well (such as cast iron, carbon steel, or stainless steel) over medium heat, cook the bacon. When the bacon is crisp and browned, use a slotted spoon to transfer it to a plate. Leave about 2 tablespoons of the bacon grease in the skillet.

Rewarm the pan over high heat. When it is just shy of smoking, add half of the green beans, spreading them out to fry and sear for 1 to 2 minutes, stirring occasionally, until lightly browned and blistered here and there; some dark brown patches are okay too. Transfer to the plate with the bacon and repeat with the remaining green beans.

/ CONTINUED

Return the first batch of green beans and the bacon to the skillet, dump in the garlic, and cook, stirring, until hot, 30 to 60 seconds. Splash in the seasoning liquid and cook for about 30 seconds, until the liquid has evaporated.

Heap the green beans onto a serving plate and enjoy.

NOTES /

The parboiled and cooled beans can be kept in an airtight container in the refrigerator for up to 3 days. Return to room temperature and pat dry before continuing with the recipe.

To make a **meatless version with a bacon substitute**, parboil the beans as directed, then drain and cool. For a vegetarian seasoning sauce, mix together ⅛ teaspoon five-spice powder, ⅛ teaspoon fine sea salt, 2 teaspoons soy sauce, and 2 teaspoons maple syrup (or honey and water). Cut up 3 or 4 slices vegetarian bacon and fry in 2 tablespoons canola or other neutral oil, and continue with the recipe.

Or, take the beans in a different direction by subbing Lemongrass Tempeh Crumbles (page 155) for the bacon. Parboil the green beans, drain, and cool, then blister them as instructed in 2 tablespoons neutral oil. Add 3 to 4 tablespoons of crumbles with the garlic. Use the above vegetarian seasoning sauce.

BABY KALE STIR-FRIED with garlic

SERVES 4

TAKES 10 MINUTES

About 2 teaspoons oyster
sauce, plus more as needed

1 teaspoon fish sauce

1 teaspoon canola or
other neutral oil, plus
1 tablespoon

½ teaspoon sugar (optional)

1 Fresno, jalapeño, or serrano
chile, seeded and chopped
(optional)

2 large garlic cloves,
finely chopped

1 teaspoon cornstarch

2 teaspoons water

Two 5- to 6-ounce packages
prewashed baby kale,
spinach, or a blend of
leafy greens

Recently ground black pepper

The go-to leafy green vegetable in Vietnam is water spinach (*rau muống* in Vietnamese; *on choy* in Cantonese). The spear-shaped leaves and tender stems have a delicate, grassy flavor and are often stir-fried with garlic and oyster sauce for a silky, earthy side dish reminiscent of creamed spinach.

I've long suggested regular spinach as a substitute for stir-fried water spinach, but lately I've switched to prewashed baby greens (kale, spinach, or a blend); they cook up quickly and don't release much liquid, which dilutes flavors. The young greens have a mild taste similar to water spinach and they don't require much prep. This side dish is great with Vietnamese food (such as the oven-steamed eggs on page 147) as well as roasted or grilled chicken or salmon. Include the chile for color and textural pop, if you like.

/

In a small bowl, combine the oyster sauce, fish sauce, and 1 teaspoon canola oil. Taste and add additional oyster sauce if you like briny depth (I often need an extra 1 teaspoon when I use Dynasty brand); if you want some sweetness to balance the flavor, add the sugar. Add the chile (if using) and about one-third of the garlic and stir to mix. Set the flavoring sauce near the stove. Mix the cornstarch with the water, then set the slurry by the stove too, along with the kale.

In a 5- to 6-quart Dutch oven or a large sauté pan over high heat, warm the remaining 1 tablespoon canola oil. When the oil is shimmering, add the remaining garlic and stir-fry for 5 to 10 seconds, until fragrant. Add one-fourth of the greens and stir and fold a few times. As soon as they soften and collapse, add another one-fourth. Repeat until all the greens are in the pan. When the greens are about one-third of their original volume, stir the flavoring sauce and add to the pan. (The greens will collapse more.)

Quickly stir and fold to distribute the sauce evenly. When the greens have released their juices, add the cornstarch slurry and cook for 30 seconds, until the sauce thickens slightly and the greens take on a silky, shiny finish.

Transfer the kale to a plate, sprinkle with pepper, and serve.

EASY SOY SAUCE–GLAZED zucchini

SERVES 4

TAKES 15 MINUTES

1 pound zucchini

½ teaspoon fine sea salt

2 teaspoons canola or other neutral oil

1 garlic clove, smashed

1½ teaspoons soy sauce, Bragg Liquid Aminos, or Maggi Seasoning sauce

1 teaspoon chile garlic sauce (see page 31) or sambal oelek (optional)

Vietnamese cooks often salt, rinse, and squeeze vegetables for salads and pickles. Why? It concentrates flavors by removing excess liquid, which allows the vegetables to really absorb a dressing or brine. I use that same approach on zucchini (medium ones work great), which can get mushy and lifeless during the cooking process. Pre-salting results in tasty, tender-firm squash, which takes on seasonings well during a quick session in a hot pan. To apply this cooking method to sunburst (aka pattypan) squash, halve them and then cut into ¾-inch-thick wedges.

A splash of soy sauce injects umami while imparting rich color. If the accompanying dishes are mild, throw in some chile garlic sauce or sambal oelek too.

/

Trim the ends off each zucchini, halve the zucchini lengthwise, and cut crosswise or on the diagonal into half circles or half oblongs, each about ¼ inch thick. Transfer to a medium bowl and toss with the salt. Set aside for 10 minutes, until there's a small pool of water in the bottom of the bowl.

Dump the zucchini into a strainer or colander and rinse with cool water for 5 to 10 seconds to remove most of the salt. Standing over the sink, squeeze by the small handful to expel a little extra water. (It's okay to leave finger impressions on the thinner pieces but don't totally crush the squash; pat with paper towels if the zucchini is still glistening with lots of moisture.)

In a large nonstick, carbon-steel, or stainless-steel skillet over medium-high or high heat, warm the canola oil. When the oil is shimmering, add the zucchini and garlic and cook, stirring frequently, for about 2 minutes, until hot and some of the zucchini pieces brown a bit. The tender-crisp zucchini should plump up and look refreshed. Splash in the soy sauce and cook, stirring vigorously and turning the zucchini to season and glaze. Plop in the chile sauce (if using), stir for 10 to 15 seconds to coat the zucchini, and then remove the pan from the heat.

Serve the zucchini warm.

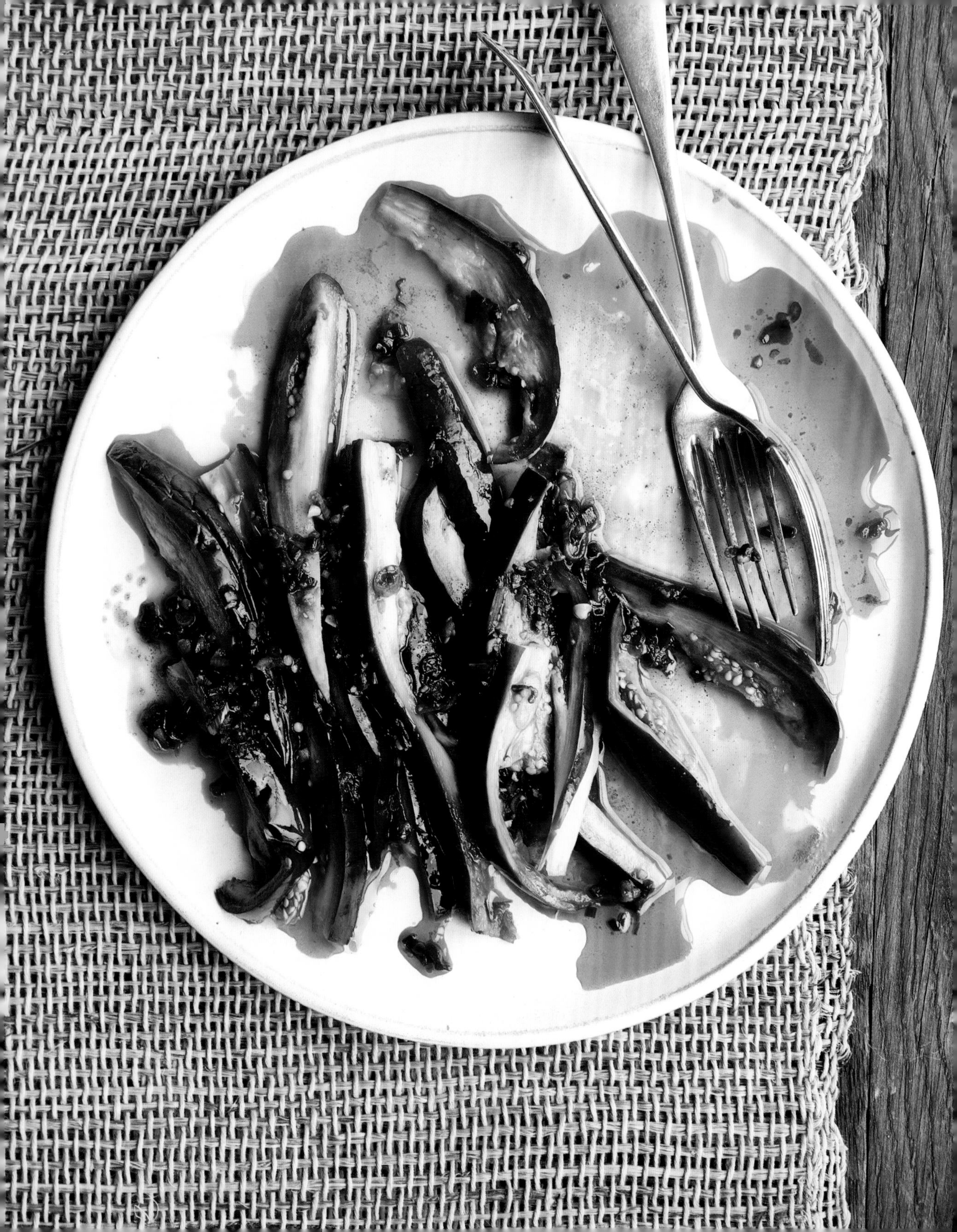

EGGPLANT with smoky green onion oil

SERVES 4

TAKES 20 MINUTES

1 medium eggplant

2½ tablespoons canola or other neutral oil

½ teaspoon smoked paprika

2 garlic cloves, finely chopped

1 tablespoon fish sauce, or scant 1½ tablespoons soy sauce

⅓ cup thinly sliced green onion, green and white parts

Fine sea salt

I typically roast whole eggplant on the stove top or an outdoor grill, remove the charred skin, and serve the soft, slightly smoky flesh with green onion oil and a dipping sauce of fish sauce and garlic, a Viet classic called *cà tím nướng mỡ hành*. When I learned that eggplant skin is loaded with antioxidants, I began thinking about how I could tweak the popular side dish to retain the skin.

Surprisingly, microwaving the entire eggplant proved to be the best way to effortlessly and evenly cook the purple orbs to a wonderful plush texture and sweet flavor. The skin is chewy-tender, and very pleasant to eat. See the Notes for a stove-top steamer method. To season with delicate sweet smokiness, I made a rich green onion topping with garlic, fish sauce, and Spanish smoked paprika (sold in the spice aisle of many markets). The result is a new rendition that's easy, healthful, and delicious in its own right.

/

Peel off the pointy flaps of the eggplant cap but leave the stem intact, then, using a fork, poke the eggplant twelve to sixteen times all over. Put the eggplant on a microwave-safe plate and microwave on high for about 6 minutes, until soft, a bit deflated looking, and cooked through (poke a knife into the thickest part). If you're unsure, cook for another minute or so. Let the eggplant sit at room temperature for 5 minutes, or until cool enough to handle.

Meanwhile, in a small saucepan over medium-low heat, warm the canola oil and smoked paprika. After 3 to 4 minutes, when the oil is fragrant, hot, and a deep orange color, add the garlic and fish sauce. Let bubble and sizzle for roughly 10 seconds to combine and lightly cook the garlic, then add the green onion, stir, and, when softened (another 10 seconds), remove from the heat. Let cool for a few minutes before tasting; if needed, add salt, a pinch at a time, to obtain a robust, savory finish. Set the sauce aside.

/ CONTINUED

Trim the stem end of the eggplant and cut the eggplant lengthwise into slices, each a good ½ inch thick. Cut each slice lengthwise into long spears as wide as your thumb. Leave as dramatic spears, or cut them crosswise to more easily maneuver. Transfer the spears to a serving plate, leaving behind the goopy liquid that the eggplant naturally releases. Top the eggplant spears with the sauce.

At the table, gently mix the eggplant and sauce to combine the flavors, and serve.

NOTES /

Select eggplants that feel solid and heavy. The skin should be smooth, glossy, and mostly blemish-free. Instead of one medium eggplant (visualize a softball with a baseball on top), use two 10-ounce ones (a tennis ball topped by a racquetball). The microwave and steam cooking times (following) are roughly the same for both sizes. Regular grocery-store eggplants are called for here, but try other kinds, such as slender Chinese eggplants; you need about one pound total. Summer is peak eggplant season.

You can cook the eggplant and sauce up to 2 days in advance, cover, and refrigerate. Return to room temperature before using; drain and warm the eggplant slightly before serving.

To steam an eggplant, trim off the stem, then cut the eggplant lengthwise into pieces a good ½ inch thick. In batches, cut-side down, steam in a basket or rack set over boiling water for about 12 minutes, until soft and cooked through. Add water to the pot as needed.

COCONUT, CURRY, AND dill mushrooms

SERVES 4

TAKES 30 MINUTES

2½ tablespoons virgin
   coconut oil

1 pound medium or large
   cremini or white mushrooms,
   dark ends trimmed

Rounded 2 tablespoons
   chopped shallot or
   yellow onion

4 garlic cloves, thinly sliced

2 teaspoons Madras-style
   curry powder (preferably
   Sun brand)

Fine sea salt

⅓ cup roughly chopped
   fresh dill or cilantro

This super-simple dish borrows a Viet cooking method called *kho*, which is traditionally done in a clay pot and often involves letting ingredients gently simmer in their natural juices. There is little fanfare or effort, but the method creates deep flavor. Recipes such as braised pork in coconut caramel sauce (see page 133) reflect the influence of classic *kho* preparations.

I came up with this mushroom version to satisfy my frequent desire to eat low- or no-meat meals. The mushrooms develop a wonderful meatiness and a terrific little sauce to mix into rice. Add Sriracha Tofu made with extra-firm tofu (see page 151) and stir-fried leafy greens or a salad for a light meal. The mushrooms are fine as part of a steak dinner too. If fresh dill and cilantro aren't available to brighten the dish at the end, use another fresh herb, such as chives.

/

In a 2-quart pot or covered casserole, combine the coconut oil, mushrooms, shallot, garlic, and curry powder. Add 2 or 3 pinches of salt and give things a gentle stir to roughly combine, then cover and set over medium heat. When you hear bubbling, turn the heat to medium-low and cook for about 15 minutes, stirring midway through the cooking time.

When the mushrooms are soft, fragrant, and have released a fair amount of liquid, uncover the pot and let simmer briskly for 2 minutes to concentrate flavors. Throw in the dill, give a stir, and then turn off the heat. Partially cover the mushrooms and let rest for 5 to 10 minutes to concentrate their flavors, then taste and season with more salt, if needed.

Present the mushrooms in the cooking vessel (if it's appropriate), or transfer to a shallow bowl. Either way, serve warm.

8

Comforting and exhilarating carbs define this recipe collection. You'll find supporting players and one-dish wonders—from fried rice and crispy crepes to stir-fried noodles and noodle bowls—all loaded with the alluring flavors of Vietnam.

RICE AND noodles

USE-IT-UP fried rice

SERVES 4 AS A SIDE DISH

TAKES ABOUT 20 MINUTES

3 cups cooked long-grain rice, such as white or brown jasmine, at room temperature (or a few minutes out of the fridge)

2 tablespoons fat, such as canola oil, peanut oil, coconut oil, rendered lard, or European-style butter

2 garlic cloves, finely chopped

1 to 1½ cups cooked leftovers, such as meat, seafood, vegetables, tofu, or tempeh (or a combination), cut or broken up into pieces the size of large peas

1 egg, beaten

1 tablespoon fish sauce, soy sauce, Bragg Liquid Aminos, or Maggi Seasoning sauce, plus more for serving

1 green onion, white and green parts, chopped

Fine sea salt

Along with banh mi and tacos, fried rice is another go-to for repurposing leftovers. It's easy to make a luxurious mound of *cơm chiên*, as long as you remember a few points: To ensure grains that don't gum up, use dry-ish, cooked rice. Make the rice up to 5 days ahead, or prepare a fresh batch (see page 26) and let it cool completely on a baking sheet.

Add-ins such as meat and vegetables should be prepped as small-ish pieces so they'll distribute well among the grains; you want every bite to be exciting. Avoid adding too many liquid seasonings or wet ingredients to the pan, or they'll overhydrate the grains instead of just lightly coating and seasoning them. Employ lots of heat and cook quickly (line up the ingredients near the stove, so you can dump them into the pan). Cook in two batches when doubling the recipe.

This fried rice can taken in many directions. Keep it sumptuous with your choice of add-ins and rich egg, or emphasize just one of them. Omit both for a great simple fried rice to pair with other dishes. You can always enliven things with the spicy vinegar in the Notes, which has more ideas.

/

Stir the rice to prevent lumps. Set with the remaining ingredients near the stove—this recipe comes together quickly.

In a large nonstick or carbon-steel skillet over medium-high or high heat, warm 1 tablespoon of the fat. When the fat is nearly shimmering, add the garlic and stir-fry for 10 to 15 seconds, until aromatic. Add the leftovers and cook, stirring, for 1 to 2 minutes to reheat and refresh. Add the rice and stir-fry for about 2 minutes, until warm and slightly revived.

Push the rice to the skillet's perimeter to create a 4-inch-well in the middle. Add the remaining 1 tablespoon fat to the well, pour in the egg, then pour the fish sauce around the rim of the well (onto the rice). Quickly stir-fry to break up, scramble, and work

/ CONTINUED

the golden egg bits into the rice. Add the green onion and cook for 10 to 15 seconds longer, until just wilted. Turn off the heat, taste, and season with salt, if needed.

Transfer the rice to a plate or shallow bowl. Serve with additional fish sauce, soy sauce, or Maggi Seasoning in case diners want an extra-savory punch.

NOTES /

Instead of cooked leftovers, use chopped raw meat, seafood, or veggies (try mushroom, green beans, or frozen peas or carrots, thawed). Heat 1½ tablespoons oil, add the raw ingredients, and lightly season with salt, fish sauce (or soy sauce, Bragg, or Maggi). When cooked through and hot, add the rice and continue as directed.

To gild the lily with bacon, chop 2 or 3 slices, fry them up until crisp, and use the rendered fat instead of the oil. Keep the bacon in the pan as you fry the rice or use it at the end as a garnish.

To make a quick **chile garlic vinegar**, in a small bowl or jar, combine 1 sliced jalapeño with seeds intact, 1 small smashed garlic clove, 2 tablespoons unseasoned rice vinegar, and ¼ cup water and let sit for 15 minutes. Have diners use a spoon to sprinkle it over their rice. The vinegar will keep for up to 2 weeks at room temperature or for up to 1 month in the refrigerator.

CRAB AND COCONUT *fried rice*

SERVES 4 AS A SIDE DISH

TAKES 10 MINUTES

3 cups cooked long-grain
white rice, such as jasmine,
at room temperature
(or a few minutes out of
the fridge)

2 tablespoons virgin
coconut oil

1 large garlic clove, minced

½ cup packed cooked
crabmeat, such as jumbo
lump crabmeat

Scant ¼ teaspoon recently
ground black pepper

1 to 1½ teaspoons fish sauce

1 green onion, white and
green parts, thinly sliced

2 to 3 cilantro sprigs

I swooned the first time I tasted this rice, a specialty of Phu Quoc island, off the coast of Vietnam. It was presented as a dome of white grains seasoned with touches of garlic and crab. The dish had a mysterious tropical sweet note, which I later figured out was due to one stealth ingredient: Virgin coconut oil.

Over the years, I've made the island's version of *cơm rang cua* countless times to wow family and friends. For grains that separate and fry up beautifully, use room-temperature or slightly cold cooked rice that's on the dry-ish side (see the Perfect Rice recipe on page 26 for tips). Warm or soft rice yields gummy results. White rice allows the delicate flavors to shine beautifully. The cooked lump crabmeat sold in small tubs in the refrigerated seafood section is perfect here.

/

Stir the rice to prevent lumps. Set with the remaining ingredients near the stove—this recipe comes together quickly.

In a large nonstick or well-seasoned carbon-steel skillet over medium-high heat, melt 1 tablespoon of the coconut oil. When the oil is hot, add the garlic and cook for 10 to 15 seconds, until aromatic. (Remove the pan from the heat if you fear the garlic will burn.) Add the crab and pepper, stir to combine, and toss in the fish sauce (use the smaller quantity if the crab is well salted). When fragrant in a funky-good sort of way, add the green onion and give things a stir, then remove from the heat and transfer to a plate.

In the same skillet over medium-high heat, melt the remaining 1 tablespoon coconut oil. Add the rice and cook, stirring, until the rice is hot and the grains are separate, about 1 minute, then return the crab and cook for 15 to 30 seconds to combine the flavors.

Transfer the rice to a serving plate, garnish with the cilantro, and serve.

VIBRANT TURMERIC coconut rice

SERVES 4

TAKES 40 MINUTES

1½ cups long-grain white rice, such as jasmine

1¾ cups coconut water

1½ teaspoons grated peeled fresh turmeric, or ¼ teaspoon plus ⅛ teaspoon ground turmeric

¼ teaspoon fine sea salt

1½ tablespoons virgin coconut oil

For decades I've been chasing this turmeric-stained rice perfumed with coconut, trying to figure out an unfussy way to make it well. Fancy versions of *cơm nị* call for frying the rice first and cooking it with coconut milk, clove, star anise, and cinnamon, but those additions tend to muddle the flavors. Plus, coconut milk can weigh down rice and turn it gummy.

Turns out that the key is using *coconut water*, a tropical ingredient that, in recent years, has become incredibly popular in America. During cooking, the coconut water hydrates the rice without overwhelming the grains, and it imparts a delicate, sweet tropical lilt. If available, grate fresh turmeric for extra vibrancy. Coconut oil delivers the rich closing punch. This rice is often served with curries like the chicken recipe on page 101, but I've found it's also terrific with grilled meats (see the photo on page 130), seafood, and vegetables. I pack leftovers for a cheery lunch.

/

Wash the rice in several changes of water (see page 26) and drain well.

In a medium saucepan over high heat, combine the rice, coconut water, turmeric, and salt and bring to a boil, stirring occasionally to loosen the grains. Lower the heat slightly and let bubble for a few minutes, stirring occasionally. When the rice is glossy on top, turn the heat to low, cover, and cook for 10 minutes.

Turn off the heat and let the rice sit for 10 minutes. Uncover, add the coconut oil, and fluff with chopsticks or a fork to combine and to circulate the grains. Re-cover and let rest for 10 minutes, or up to 30 minutes to finish cooking. Before serving, fluff the rice again.

Transfer the rice to a serving bowl or platter and let diners help themselves.

GRATITUDE CHICKEN AND *celery rice*

SERVES 6 AS A SIDE DISH

TAKES 1 HOUR

2 cups long-grain white rice, such as jasmine

About 2¼ cups chicken stock (see page 36) or store-bought chicken broth

About 1 tablespoon fish sauce, plus more as needed

4½ tablespoons rendered chicken fat or neutral oil, or a combination

4 large celery stalks, cut on the diagonal into ⅛- to ¼-inch-thick pieces

1¼ cups shredded cooked chicken (use leftovers from making stock or a roast chicken)

Fine sea salt

Recently ground black pepper

Chicken is pricey in Vietnam. When my family arrived in the United States and discovered a wealth of cheap chicken backs, we simmered them for stock, harvested the meat and fat (schmaltz), then used those elements for this delectable but humble rice. Even when I use oil and canned broth, the tasty results still embody the comforts of Viet cooking and our gratitude for being in America.

/

Wash the rice in several changes of water (see page 26) and drain in a mesh strainer set over a bowl for about 20 minutes. Meanwhile, pour the chicken stock into a small saucepan and season with the fish sauce. (The amount used depends on the stock and your palate. I use about 1 tablespoon with homemade stock.) Bring the stock to a simmer, cover, and lower the heat to keep hot.

In a large saucepan over medium heat, warm 3 tablespoons of the rendered fat. When the fat is barely shimmering, shake the rice to expel any lingering water, dump into the pan, and lightly fry for 3 to 5 minutes, until the grains looks dry-ish and feel light under your spatula (expect some chalky grains). Add the hot stock, stir, and briefly let it bubble and sizzle, then adjust the heat to medium-low, cover the pot, and cook for 2 to 4 minutes, lifting the lid occasionally to stir. When liquid is barely visible and a few craters form at the top of the rice, turn the heat to low, cover, and cook for 10 minutes more.

Meanwhile, in a medium skillet over medium heat, warm the remaining 1½ tablespoons rendered fat. Add the celery and cook for about 2 minutes, until jade-green and slightly softened. Add the chicken and cook for 1 to 2 minutes to heat through. Remove from the heat, then season with salt and pepper and perhaps a sprinkle of fish sauce too.

Turn off the heat under the rice, uncover, and add the celery and chicken, spreading them on top. Replace the lid and let sit for 10 minutes to continue cooking. Use a fork to fluff the rice and stir in the celery and chicken. (If the rice is dry, add 1 to 2 tablespoons water.) Re-cover and let rest for 10 minutes more. Before serving, fluff the rice again, taste, and tweak with salt, pepper, or fish sauce. Transfer the rice to a serving bowl or platter and place on the table.

SIZZLING RICE crepes

**MAKES 6 CREPES,
TO SERVE 3 OR 4**

TAKES ABOUT 1½ HOURS

BATTER

4¼ ounces white rice flour
(such as Bob's Red Mill)

1 tablespoon cornstarch

½ teaspoon fine sea salt

¼ teaspoon plus ⅛ teaspoon
ground turmeric

¾ cup tepid water mixed
with ¾ cup freshly
boiled water (rest boiled
water 1 minute and then
measure), plus more water
as needed

⅓ cup full-fat unsweetened
coconut milk (shake or stir
before using)

FILLING

10 ounces ground pork
(85% lean), chicken thigh,
or beef chuck, roughly
chopped to loosen

8 ounces small shrimp,
peeled and deveined

4 medium white mushrooms
or fresh shiitake
mushrooms, thinly sliced,
stems included

½ small red or yellow onion,
thinly sliced

Fine sea salt

3 cups bean sprouts

These crepes are yellow and folded over like an omelet, but don't contain eggs; they're crisp like the bottom of a paella, but no rice grains are visible. *Bánh xèo* rice crepes are in a class of their own. The southern Viet charmers are named for the sizzling sound they make while cooking and typically contain pork, shrimp, mushroom, and bean sprouts. Snipped or broken into pieces and eaten as lettuce-and-herb wraps with *nước chấm* dipping sauce, the crepes hit all pleasure centers.

For years, I soaked and ground raw rice or used its equivalent, Thai rice flour, to make velvety batters. Supermarket white rice flour yielded gritty results until I tried making the batter with super-hot water. Bingo! The rice starch softened enough to yield finer textured crepes. Compared to the traditional ones, these are crunchier and heartier—and wonderfully delicious in their own right. Weigh the flour for precision, but play with the filling. Use sliced red cabbage when beans sprouts are unavailable or look sad. See the Notes for a meatless option.

Cook the crepes in a nonstick or well-seasoned carbon-steel skillet (cast iron will make it hard to swirl the batter; use two skillets for efficiency). Fry/steam/fry is the approach, so be ready to adjust the heat. If available, use a burner with about 12,000 BTUs to ensure sufficient heat. Set up a DIY crepe station for a fun party.

/

To make the batter In a medium bowl, whisk together the rice flour, cornstarch, salt, and turmeric. Whisk in the water and then the coconut milk. Let the yellow batter sit, uncovered, for 30 to 45 minutes, to thicken to the consistency of half-and-half (it will be slightly gritty from the flour). Whisk in more water, 1 teaspoon at a time, to thin out the batter, if needed (when I have to add water, it's usually no more than 1 tablespoon). The batter may be made up to 2 days ahead and stored, covered, in the refrigerator; bring to room temperature before using.

To prep the filling In order to cook efficiently with less mess, pre-portion the filling components. Divide the pork, shrimp,

/ CONTINUED

Canola or other neutral oil
for cooking

Leaves from 1 large head
soft-leaf lettuce (such as
butter, Boston, or red or
green leaf)

1 small handful mint, basil, or
other soft-leaf fresh herbs
(except cilantro)

1 small handful cilantro

1 cup Nuoc Cham Dipping
Sauce (page 30)

mushrooms, and onion onto six small pieces of parchment paper, creating a pile of goodies for each crepe. Sprinkle each portion with a pinch of salt. Set on a tray or baking sheet and keep near the stove with the batter and bean sprouts.

Place a large cooling rack on a baking sheet for the cooked crepes. Preheat the oven to Warm or to its lowest setting.

To fry the crepes In a medium nonstick skillet over medium-high heat, warm 2 to 3 teaspoons of the canola oil. When the oil is very hot and shimmering, add a portion of filling and stir-fry for 45 seconds, breaking up the meat with a spatula until it no longer looks raw; the mushrooms will probably look moist. Make a line down the middle to divide the ingredients into two half-circles; this will ensure the crepe later folds over easily. Lower the heat slightly if you feel things are out of control; you can always turn it up later!

Stir the batter vigorously with a ladle until there is no more drag, sludge, or separation. Scoop up about ⅓ cup batter and pour into the skillet, distributing it around the filling. Pick up the skillet and swirl the batter to coat the bottom (and maybe run up the sides); the batter should set around the filling and form a handsome round. If needed, add more batter to quickly fill in empty spots. (If the batter didn't sizzle and bubble upon contact, the skillet wasn't hot enough. If it did bubble but was hard to swirl around, lower the heat or thin out the batter with water, or do both. Making these crepes is akin to making pancakes: adjust as you go.)

Pile about ¾ cup bean sprouts on one side of the skillet, lower the heat slightly, and cover the pan with a lid to steam; if it's a tight fit, slide the lid so it's ajar to allow a bit of venting. Cook for 2 to 3 minutes, until the bean sprouts soften slightly, then uncover the pan and drizzle 1 to 2 teaspoons oil around the rim. Lower the heat again (I'm typically at medium at this point) to gently fry and crisp, 3 to 4 minutes. When the crepe is golden brown at the edge, use a spatula to peek underneath. Is it mostly crisp from the rim to the center? If not, fry a little longer; and if needed, add oil and raise the heat. Be patient. When you're satisfied, slide a spatula under one side and lift to fold the crepe over. No big deal if it breaks in the center.

Slide the finished crepe onto the prepared rack and hold in the oven, or if serving immediately, transfer to a dinner plate. Rewarm the skillet over medium-high heat and repeat the whole process to make another five crepes. If at any time the batter feels too thick, add water, 1 teaspoon at a time, to thin it out. If you have two medium skillets, use both like a pro to speed things up.

Serve the crepes with the lettuce, herbs, cilantro, and dipping sauce. Pass around one or two pairs of kitchen scissors to cut the crepes into manageable pieces. To eat, tear a piece of lettuce roughly the size of your palm, place a piece of the crepe on it, and add a few herb leaves. Fold into a bundle and dunk into the dipping sauce.

NOTE /

For **meatless crepes**, replace the meat and shrimp with 5 ounces of thinly sliced Sriracha Tofu made with extra-firm tofu (see the Notes on page 151); or, crumble 8 ounces tempeh and season with 1 teaspoon soy sauce and ¼ teaspoon salt. Increase the number of mushrooms to six. Serve with vegetarian or regular Nuoc Cham Dipping Sauce plus the usual lettuce and herbs.

UMAMI GARLIC NOODLES with shiitake mushroom

SERVES 4

TAKES ABOUT 40 MINUTES

4 large garlic cloves, minced or put through a press

10 ounces dried Chinese wheat noodles or Japanese ramen

Fine sea salt

1 tablespoon oyster sauce

2 teaspoons fish sauce

1 teaspoon cornstarch

½ teaspoon MSG, scant ½ teaspoon chicken stock base, or 2 tablespoons nutritional yeast flakes

½ teaspoon sugar

4 tablespoons salted, European-style butter

8 fresh shiitake mushroom or cremini mushrooms, sliced ⅛ to ¼ inch thick, stems included

Recently ground black pepper

1 tablespoon minced shallot

A cult favorite among Viet Americans, buttery garlic noodles are addictively good, but their garlicky flavor can linger the morning after. You don't have to worry about that with this recipe. To prevent the garlic from ruining a date night (and from burning during cooking), let it hang out for a few minutes in a little water and then gently cook it.

Using salted European-style butter, such as Kerrygold, is my nod to the Viet penchant for Bretel, a canned cultured butter from Normandy, which the French introduced to Vietnam. Liquid seasonings such as oyster sauce and fish sauce support and build on the butter's umami goodness; see the Notes for vegetarian substitutes. To send the flavors over the top, add a glutamate-rich flavor enhancer. If you are someone who isn't skittish about MSG, use it here to great effect. Top the noodles with seared large shrimp to fancy them up. Add a simple vegetable dish or green salad to complete the meal.

/

Fill a large pot with 4 quarts water and bring to a boil.

Meanwhile, put the garlic in a small cup or dish and add about 1 tablespoon water to just barely cover. Set aside and expect the garlic to absorb most of the water; there is no need to drain it before adding later.

After the pot comes to a boil, add the noodles and 2 teaspoons salt. Boil the noodles until just chewy-firm; they'll soften more later. Ladle out ¾ cup of the cooking liquid. Drain the noodles in a colander, rinse with cool water, and set aside. In a small bowl, whisk together the oyster sauce, fish sauce, cornstarch, MSG, sugar, and reserved cooking water. Set aside.

If the pot that you cooked the noodles in is wide enough to comfortably sauté the mushrooms, set it over medium-high heat and melt 2 tablespoons of the butter; if not, use a large skillet. Add the mushrooms, season with 2 or 3 pinches of salt and pepper, and cook, stirring, for 2 to 3 minutes, until the mushrooms start to brown. Turn off the heat and transfer the mushrooms to a plate or bowl.

RICE NOODLE salad bowl

SERVES 4

TAKES ABOUT 1½ HOURS

MARINADE

3 garlic cloves, chopped

½ cup coarsely chopped
shallot or yellow onion

¼ teaspoon plus ⅛ teaspoon
recently ground black
pepper

½ teaspoon Chinese
five-spice powder

1½ tablespoons granulated
sugar, or 2 tablespoons
packed light brown sugar

½ teaspoon molasses, dark
amber honey, or Caramel
Sauce (page 32)

1½ tablespoons fish sauce

1 teaspoon soy sauce

1½ tablespoons canola or
other neutral oil, plus more
for grilling

1¼ pounds well-marbled
beefsteak (such as tri-tip
or New York strip steak),
boneless pork shoulder,
boneless country-style
pork ribs, or boneless,
skinless chicken thigh

One 6- to 8-ounce package
small dried round rice
noodles (maifun), or one
10- to 12-ounce package
dried rice capellini or thin
spaghetti (see page 15)

1 cup Nuoc Cham Dipping
Sauce (page 30)

Like banh mi sandwiches, southern Viet rice noodle salad bowls are adaptable and great for healthful, impromptu meals. Often categorized at restaurants as rice vermicelli bowls or *bún* (the name of the noodles), they're built on this blueprint: A large bowl filled with ribbons of lettuce and a thin, crunchy vegetable for texture; fresh herbs for pungency; and slippery rice noodles to convey flavors. You get to choose the toppings, which are inevitably garnished with roasted peanuts. A fancy bowl often has pickled radish and carrot for color and crunch, plus fried shallots for extra richness (canned fried onions are my lazy-day sub). You dress the bowl with *nước chấm* dipping sauce, toss it with chopsticks (or a fork) and spoon, and then dive in.

To quickly make your own, keep some dried noodles on hand as well as a jar of *nước chấm* sauce base (see the Note on page 30), washed herbs and lettuce or baby lettuce mix (see page 19 for storage information), and roasted nuts. All that's left is the main attraction. Following is a versatile marinade for beef, pork, and chicken skewers. In the Notes you'll find more ideas to fuel your creativity.

To grill the meat, you will need skewers. With 6-inch skewers, you'll fill eight to ten of them; with 10-inch ones, you'll need four or five skewers.

/

If using wooden skewers and intending to cook over a live fire, soak them in hot water for 20 minutes.

To make the marinade In a small food processor, combine the garlic, shallot, pepper, five-spice powder, sugar, molasses, fish sauce, soy sauce, and canola oil, then whirl into a slightly coarse, liquid-y marinade. (Or, pound the garlic, shallot, and sugar with a mortar and pestle and mix in the other ingredients.) Transfer the marinade to a large bowl.

/ CONTINUED

⅔ cup unsalted roasted peanuts or cashew pieces, coarsely chopped if large

¼ cup fried onions or shallots (optional)

4 cups baby lettuce mix or leaves of soft-leaf lettuce (such as butter, Boston, or green leaf), cut into narrow ribbons, with spines intact

3 or 4 handfuls bean sprouts, or 1 Persian cucumber, shaved with a vegetable peeler into thin strips, or both

½ cup hand-torn fresh cilantro leaves and tender tops

½ cup hand-torn fresh mint leaves, basil leaves, or dill fronds, or a combination

½ to ¾ cup Any Day Viet Pickle (page 29; optional, but encouraged for extra dimension)

If using beef or pork, cut the meat across the grain into strips about 1 inch wide, 3 inches long, and a scant ¼ inch thick. If using chicken, cut each thigh crosswise into 1-inch-wide strips; if a thigh is super-thick on one end, cut one or two gashes there to even out the thickness before cutting the strips. Add to the marinade, and massage to coat well.

Thread the meat onto the skewers, covering most of each skewer. For succulence, give each loaded skewer a gentle squeeze to ensure that the meat hugs the skewer. Set on a plate, cover, and let marinate at room temperature for 30 to 60 minutes.

Meanwhile, in a pot of unsalted water, boil the noodles until tender; the cooking time depends on the noodle and brand. Drain in a colander, rinse with cold water, and set aside to drain well. Put the dipping sauce in a serving bowl. Set the nuts and fried onions (if using) near the stove.

Divide the lettuce and bean sprouts among four large soup or pasta bowls (you'll need room later to mix and toss). Add the cilantro and mint, reserving 2 tablespoons for garnish. Top with a layer of noodles. Tuck a small pile of pickle (if using) into each bowl. Set near the stove.

Right before grilling, lightly spray or brush oil on the meat. Lightly oil a cast-iron stove-top grill pan and set over medium-high heat. Or, prepare a medium-hot charcoal fire or preheat a gas grill to medium-high (you can hold your hand 6 inches above the grill for 3 or 4 seconds).

Cook the skewers for 8 to 12 minutes, turning frequently and basting with oil, until the meat is slightly charred and cooked through. Nick a piece with the point of a knife to check. Divide the meat among the bowls, either keeping it on the skewers or sliding it off. Crown with the nuts, fried onions, and reserved herbs.

Serve the bowls with the sauce on the side. Have diners dress and toss their own bowls.

NOTES /

Metal skewers won't burn up, but wooden (bamboo) ones are handsome. If you choose wood ones, buy sturdy flat or thick round skewers. They have a higher tolerance for heat, won't bend or droop once loaded, and can be snipped with scissors to fit a stove-top grill pan.

In a pinch, cook the skewers in a cast-iron skillet. The cooking time will be shorter.

The marinade can be made and the noodles can be boiled up to 3 days in advance and refrigerated in separate airtight containers. Before using the noodles, sprinkle a little water on them and microwave on high for 60 to 90 seconds, until soft and refreshed.

To add shrimp to a bowl, peel and devein 8 extra-large or 12 large shrimp, season with salt and pepper, and coat with a little oil. Grill them along with the skewers. For a **seafood bowl**, top with grilled trout (see page 119) or lemongrass salmon (see page 117) instead of meat.

For a **vegetarian bowl**, top with the Sriracha Tofu on page 150 (thinly slice it if you used extra-firm tofu), grilled vegetables, and seared mushrooms (slice portobellos or cremini and sear in a very hot skillet with a bit of oil and sprinklings of salt and pepper; when soft and glistening, splash with soy sauce for a savory burst, if you like). Dress with vegetarian or regular Nuoc Cham Dipping Sauce.

And consider featuring Grilled Slashed Chicken (page 98), Grilled Lemongrass Pork Chops (page 131), or curry-scented grilled beef (see page 139). Cut them into bite-size pieces, as needed. Or, slice up leftover steak or roasts and quickly sauté the meat in a hot pan with a splash of oil, minced garlic, and chopped shallot (or onion) to make a quick topping.

CRAB AND BLACK PEPPER *glass noodles*

SERVES 4 AS A SIDE DISH

TAKES 20 MINUTES

3½ ounces dried glass noodles (saifun or bean thread noodles; see page 14)

1 egg, plus 1 egg yolk

Scant ¾ teaspoon recently ground black pepper

1½ tablespoons fish sauce

2 tablespoons lightly packed finely chopped fresh cilantro, stems included

2 tablespoons canola or other neutral oil

½ cup thinly sliced shallot or small red or yellow onion

1½ medium celery stalks, very thinly sliced on the diagonal

¾ cup packed cooked crabmeat, such as jumbo lump crabmeat

3 or 4 cilantro sprigs (optional)

Called *miến xào cua* in Vietnamese, this easy, though luxurious, noodle dish highlights the remarkable qualities of *saifun*, chewy-tender noodles made of mung bean starch. When soaked in water and then cooked with egg, fish sauce, and lots of black pepper—a combination that fabulously mimics the richness and brininess of crab tomalley—the noodles turn clear, like glass, and plump up as they become infused with crablike flavor. Cooked crab reinforces the briny richness that the noodles convey and celery adds delicate crunch and color.

If you pick the meat from a cooked crab for this dish, use the crab fat (tomalley) to replace the egg yolk. I often use the refrigerated jumbo lump crabmeat sold in small tubs, with excellent results; you need only six ounces. Canned crabmeat lacks good flavor, and surimi, which is an imitation, is rubbery. Resist using them.

/

Soak the noodles in hot water for 5 to 10 minutes, until pliable, then drain, cut with scissors into 10-inch lengths, and set aside.

In a measuring cup, combine the egg, egg yolk, pepper, fish sauce, and cilantro. Add water to make ¾ cup, then mix well with a fork to create a seasoning liquid. Set near the stove with the remaining ingredients.

In a large nonstick skillet over medium heat, warm the canola oil. Add the shallot and cook, stirring, for about 2 minutes, until soft. Then, add the celery and crabmeat and cook for about 1 minute, until aromatic and the celery looks jadelike and is slightly soft. Add the noodles and cook, stirring, for 1 to 2 minutes, until they begin to soften. Lower the heat slightly, give the seasoning liquid a good stir, and pour over the noodles. Quickly stir and gently fold the mixture into the noodles to evenly distribute the flavors. In 1 to 2 minutes, the noodles will become translucent, plump, and pale golden. Remove from the heat.

Transfer the noodles to a plate and garnish with the cilantro sprigs. Serve warm.

HANOI-STYLE BACON AND
grilled pork rice noodle bowls

SERVES 4

TAKES 1¼ HOURS

One 6- to 8-ounce package small dried round rice noodles (maifun), or one 10- to 12-ounce package dried rice capellini or thin spaghetti (see page 15)

1 cup Nuoc Cham Dipping Sauce (page 30)

⅔ cup water

1 small carrot, thinly sliced or shaved with a vegetable peeler

1 small kohlrabi, peeled, halved, and thinly sliced or shaved with a vegetable peeler (optional)

Leaves from 1 large head soft-leaf lettuce (such as butter, Boston, or red or green leaf)

1 small handful mint or basil sprigs, or a combination

1 small handful cilantro sprigs

½ cup chopped shallot or yellow onion

2½ tablespoons fish sauce

2 tablespoons canola or other neutral oil, plus more for grilling

2½ teaspoons Caramel Sauce (page 32), or 2 teaspoons molasses

1 tablespoon plus ¾ teaspoon sugar

Whereas in and around Saigon, people love to dig into bodacious bowls of *bún* rice noodle salads (see page 197), Hanoians adore leisurely meals of *bún chả*, which involves composing and enjoying smallish bowls of lettuce, herbs, rice noodles, and grilled pork. The former delivers convenience in a bowl, the latter coaxes conversation. They use the same ingredients, but Hanoi cooks do something quirky—they plunge the grilled meat into the dipping sauce, where it releases its juices to build extra umami depth. Thin slices of carrot and kohlrabi marinate in the sauce to add a pickled crunch.

In Hanoi, two kinds of pork are typically cooked over charcoal; ground pork patties and sliced fatty pork or pork belly. For the sliced pork, I bake bacon, which lends a smoky, rich flavor. I cook the patties on a stove-top cast-iron grill. There's less work involved to create this delicious signature dish of Hanoi. For extra authenticity points, see the Notes for details on swapping pork shoulder for bacon.

/

In a pot of unsalted water, boil the noodles until chewy-tender; the cooking time depends on the noodle and brand. Drain in a colander, rinse with cold water, and drain well for about 5 minutes. For easy serving, arrange the noodles as 2- to 3-inch nests on two plates or in low bowls.

Dilute the dipping sauce with the ⅔ cup water. Divide among two soup bowls for sharing or four cereal bowls for individual servings (bowls with a capacity of 2 to 3 cups work well). Divide the carrot and kohlrabi (if using) among the bowls. Set aside. Arrange the lettuce and herbs on two platters and set on the table with the rice noodles. For each diner, set out a cereal or rice bowl, plus chopsticks (or a fork) and a spoon.

Preheat the oven to 400°F. Line a large rimmed baking sheet with aluminum foil and set aside.

/ CONTINUED

Scant 1 teaspoon recently ground black pepper

12 ounces mildly salty bacon, regular or thick-cut (see Note)

1¼ pounds ground pork (about 85% lean)

¼ teaspoon fine sea salt

In a small food processor, combine the shallot, fish sauce, canola oil, caramel sauce, sugar, and pepper and whirl into a slightly coarse puree. (Or, use a mortar and pestle to pound the shallot, sugar, and pepper into a rough paste and then add the liquid ingredients).

Pour ¼ cup of the puree into a medium bowl, add the bacon, and massage to coat each bacon slice well. Arrange the bacon on the prepared baking sheet; lay the slices flat and let them touch. Bake for 16 to 18 minutes for regular cut, or 23 to 25 minutes for thick cut, until well browned and chewy-crisp. Let cool on paper towels to drain and finish crisping. For easier eating, cut or snip the bacon strips crosswise into 3-inch pieces.

Meanwhile, in a medium bowl, combine the ground pork, salt, and 1½ tablespoons puree, reserving the rest. Mix well, then let sit for 5 minutes to firm up. Shape the pork into twelve patties, each about 2½ inches in diameter and a good ½ thick. For even cooking, use a finger or fat chopstick to poke a hole in the center of each one. Set aside on parchment or wax paper.

Oil a cast-iron stove-top grill pan and set over high heat. Add the patties and grill for about 6 minutes, turning frequently and basting with the remaining puree, until there are char marks and the pork is cooked through; nick a patty with the point of a knife to check. Divide the patties among the bowls with the dipping sauce and add the bacon. Set at the table with the noodles and garnishes.

To eat, have diners break each patty into three or four chunks to soak up the sauce. Tear the lettuce and herbs leaves into manageable-size pieces, dropping them into individual bowls. Top with a mound of noodles, add the bacon and patty pieces, and drizzle with sauce, including the pickled carrot and kohlrabi for crunch. Mix things up, and eat. Repeat until everything is gone.

NOTES /

Mildly salty bacon has about 170 mg of sodium per two-slice serving. It may or may not be labeled "low sodium." If you don't eat pork, use turkey bacon and ground turkey thigh.

To serve this in a flash, prep the noodles, sauce, and marinade up to 3 days in advance and store, covered, in the refrigerator. To soften and refresh the noodles, sprinkle with some water and then microwave them on high for 60 to 90 seconds.

Instead of the bacon, use 12 ounces fatty pork shoulder or boneless country-style pork ribs. Cut the meat into strips 3 to 4 inches long, 1 inch wide, and ¼ inch thick. Marinate for 1 hour, or up to overnight. To maximize browning and savory depth, grill the pork pieces for about 2 minutes, turning frequently. Or, sear them in a super-hot, lightly oiled skillet.

A NIFTY TRICK FOR DRAINING NOODLES

To prevent noodles from sticking together too much, invert a small bowl in the bottom of the colander before draining. The cooked noodles will surround and drape over the bowl instead of meeting in the middle.

TURMERIC FISH, SEARED DILL, AND
green onion noodle bowls

SERVES 4

TAKES ABOUT 1¼ HOURS

2 pounds catfish or tilapia fillets

1 tablespoon packed finely grated peeled fresh turmeric, or 1½ teaspoons ground turmeric

2 teaspoons finely grated peeled fresh ginger or galangal

1½ tablespoons anchovy paste

1½ teaspoons fish sauce

⅓ cup sour cream

2 tablespoons canola oil, plus ¼ cup

Brimming ½ cup chopped fresh dill fronds

3 green onions, white and green parts, thinly sliced

DIPPING SAUCE

1 tablespoon anchovy paste

3 tablespoons sugar

⅓ cup fresh lime juice

3 tablespoons fish sauce

¼ cup water

1 to 2 teaspoons unseasoned rice vinegar (optional)

2 Thai chiles, or 1 serrano chile, thinly sliced, with seeds intact (optional)

Like the pork and rice noodle bowls on page 201, turmeric-stained *chả cá Hà Nội* is a superb and iconic dish from Vietnam's capital. Finding supermarket ingredients to make this treat required creativity, because it typically features pieces of freshwater fish fillet marinated in a creamy, umami-laden mixture of turmeric, galangal (an edgy cousin of ginger and turmeric), fermented shrimp sauce (*mắm tôm*, a toothpaste-textured, mauve-colored umami bomb), and *mẻ* (a mash of fermented cooked rice).

The fish is cooked on a brazier, topped with green onion and dill, and then finished with a pour of hot oil to sear the aromatics. It's served with the usual suspects (noodles, lettuce, and herbs) along with roasted peanuts and crumbled toasted rice crackers, which act like croutons to add richness and crunch. A tangy, savory sauce made with shrimp and fish sauces dresses all the components for a stunning one-dish meal.

Many people point to the famous version from Chả Cá Lã Vọng restaurant in Hanoi, but you can create a fabulous rendition from regular grocery store items. Buy catfish or tilapia fillets (thick, big ones work best), swap anchovy paste for shrimp sauce, use ginger in lieu of galangal, sub sour cream for fermented cooked rice, and offer small rice cracker rounds or tortilla chips instead of larger rice crackers. Broiling the fish is much easier than squatting and fanning a brazier. With those work-arounds, there's little flavor loss as you enjoy major Viet cooking gains.

/

Pat the fish dry with paper towels. Halve each fillet lengthwise (let the backbone indentation be your guide) and then cut each fillet half into "fish fingers" roughly 4 inches long and 1 inch wide. To obtain long pieces, you may have to cut the fish at an angle, creating trapezoid-shaped pieces. Set aside.

/ CONTINUED

ACCOMPANIMENTS

One 6- to 8-ounce package dried rice noodles (maifun), or one 10- to 12-ounce package dried rice capellini or thin spaghetti (see page 15)

Leaves from 1 head soft-leaf lettuce (such as butter or Boston), or 5 to 6 cups baby lettuce mix

1 small handful mint or basil sprigs, or combination

1 small handful cilantro sprigs

½ cup unsalted roasted peanuts

1 cup plain or sesame rice crackers

In a large bowl, combine the turmeric, ginger, anchovy paste, fish sauce, sour cream, and 2 tablespoons canola oil. Add the fish and use your hands or a silicone spatula to coat the pieces evenly. Cover and set aside to marinate while you ready the other components. Set the dill, green onions, and remaining ¼ cup canola oil near the stove.

To make the dipping sauce In a small bowl, whisk together the anchovy paste, sugar, and lime juice, which will give you a pale purple mixture. Add the fish sauce and water and taste; if the sauce is a little bitter or sharp, add the vinegar, 1 teaspoon at a time. Then, add the chiles, stir, and set aside.

Position an oven rack about 4 inches from the broiler's heat source and preheat the broiler for 20 minutes. Line a baking sheet with aluminum foil and set a rack inside.

To prep the accompaniments In a pot of unsalted water, boil the noodles until chewy-tender; the cooking time depends on the noodle and brand. Drain, rinse with cool water, and drain well for about 5 minutes. For easy serving, arrange the noodles as 2- to 3-inch nests on two plates or in low bowls. Place the noodles, lettuce, herbs, peanuts, dipping sauce, and rice crackers at the table. For each diner, set out a cereal bowl or small soup bowl, chopsticks (or a fork), and a spoon.

Arrange the fish pieces on the prepared rack, laying them flat, like a jigsaw puzzle. Broil for about 8 minutes, until the fish is sizzling and a little brown; check after 5 minutes and rotate the pan, if needed. Using chopsticks, tongs, or an offset spatula, delicately loosen and turn the fish over, then broil for 5 to 8 minutes more, until tinged brown on the second side. Let cool for 3 to 5 minutes. Transfer the fish to one or two serving plates and blanket with the dill and green onions.

In a small saucepan, heat the remaining ¼ cup canola oil until faint wisps of smoke start rising. Pour the hot oil over the green onions and dill to sear and wilt them. Using two spoons, gently combine, and then place the fish on the table.

When ready to eat, diners should put some of each component in an individual bowl, tearing the lettuce and herbs into bite-size pieces and breaking up the rice crackers. Dress with a small drizzle of sauce (wield chopsticks and spoon to mix) and gobble it up. Repeat until everything is gone.

NOTES /

Anchovy paste is usually shelved near the canned seafood. (If you have *mắm tôm* fermented shrimp sauce, substitute an equal amount for the paste.) If the anchovy paste–based sauce sounds too bizarre, make a batch of Nuoc Cham Dipping Sauce (page 30) instead.

Knobby galangal (pictured on the lower right side of page 21) is sometimes carried at mainstream markets such as Whole Foods.

No large rack? Broil the fish on the foil; if liquid accumulates, make a spout in one corner of the foil, pour off the liquid, and finish broiling.

For advance prep, marinate the fish, make the sauce, boil the noodles, and wash the lettuce and herbs 1 day ahead and store, covered, in the refrigerator. To soften and refresh the noodles, sprinkle with water and microwave on high for 60 to 90 seconds.

9

Whether you're in the mood for something cool, warm, fragrant, or elegant, these sweet treats have you covered. For a beverage pairing, make Vietnamese coffee.

SWEETS
and coffee

NO-CHURN VIETNAMESE COFFEE ice cream

MAKES ABOUT 2 CUPS

TAKES 10 MINUTES, PLUS
5 TO 6 HOURS TO FREEZE

1½ to 2 teaspoons
   vanilla extract

Brimming 2 tablespoons
   instant espresso

Fine sea salt

1 cup heavy whipping cream

Brimming ⅓ cup full-fat
   sweetened condensed milk

Scant 1 tablespoon molasses

What can you make from sweetened condensed milk aside from Viet coffee drinks? Ice cream! I take a no-churn approach that involves whipping up the milk, heavy cream, and flavorings until fluffy and then freezing the mix for several hours. You don't need an ice-cream maker, just an electric handheld mixer. (An immersion blender does not add enough air.)

Instant espresso, molasses, and vanilla create a strong Vietnamese coffee flavor; brewed coffee injects too much liquid into the mixture and compromises the texture. The sea salt's edge amplifies things. If you like, gild the lily with chocolate bits (see the Note), but this ice cream is also sensational without it.

/

In a medium bowl, combine 1½ teaspoons of the vanilla, the espresso, and 2 pinches salt and stir to mix well; it will seem slightly sludgy. Add the cream, condensed milk, and molasses. Taste and, if you want to boost the flavor a touch, add more vanilla, ¼ teaspoon at a time; the amount required depends on the vanilla and your palate. An extra pinch of salt sometimes helps too.

With an electric handheld mixer fitted with two beaters or a whisk attachment, whip the mixture at high speed for about 3 minutes, until you get a firm, spreadable texture like fluffy whipped cream or frosting. Transfer to a 3- to 4-cup storage container, cover, and freeze until firm, 5 to 6 hours, or up to 2 weeks.

Let the ice cream sit at room temperature for 10 to 15 minutes to soften to a scoopable texture before serving.

NOTE /

For **coffee and chocolate ice cream**, hand chop 1½ ounces bittersweet or dark chocolate into very small bits so they will disperse well. After whipping up the ice-cream mixture, use a spatula to gently fold in the chocolate. Freeze as directed. Your yield will be a little more than the original recipe.

SILKEN TOFU AND MANDARIN ORANGES IN
ginger syrup

SERVES 4

TAKES 25 MINUTES

Chubby 1-inch (1-ounce) section ginger, peeled, very thinly sliced, and smashed

3½ tablespoons maple syrup, or 2½ tablespoons honey

¼ cup firmly packed light or dark brown sugar

¼ cup plus 1 tablespoon water

16 ounces soft silken tofu

One 11-ounce can mandarin orange segments in light syrup, drained

Warm tofu pudding served with zippy ginger syrup is one of my favorite cozy Asian desserts; it's a popular street food and a mainstay at dim sum restaurants. When freshly made tofu isn't available, I use store-bought silken tofu, available in the refrigerated section of the supermarket. Silken tofu, such as Nasoya brand that's undrained and unpressed (there is no visible water in the tub), is custardy and easy to scoop into elegant thin pieces.

With a tub of silken tofu in the fridge, I can put together *đậu hũ nước đường* in a flash. (The syrup can be made up to 5 days ahead and kept in the fridge too!) Old-school renditions feature just the tofu and syrup. Nowadays, there are new iterations with other goodies added for contrasting texture and color, much like you'd find in Asian shaved-ice concoctions. Here, the pretty and tangy mandarin orange segments pair well with the ginger and tofu.

/

In a small saucepan over medium-high heat, combine the ginger, maple syrup, brown sugar, and water and bring to a boil, stirring to dissolve the sugar. Lower the heat to simmer briskly for about 3 minutes, until fragrant and slightly thickened, then remove from the heat and let sit for 10 to 15 minutes, uncovered, to intensify in flavor and thicken more. Pour through a mesh strainer set over a small bowl, pressing on the ginger.

Wield a metal serving spoon in a horizontal motion to scoop up large, thin pieces of the tofu, dividing them among four individual serving bowls as you go along. (It's normal for the pieces to be irregular in shape and size.) Warm the bowls of tofu in the microwave. Fit as many in as possible and zap in 20-second intervals until slightly warmed through; this allows the tofu to display its tender richness. Whey will inevitably accumulate in the bowls; you may pour it out to prevent it from diluting the syrup, or just allow its delicate tanginess to add to the overall flavor.

Divide the orange segments among the bowls and pour the syrup over the top. Serve immediately.

MATCHA "PANDAN" waffles

MAKES 2 WAFFLES,
TO SERVE 4

TAKES 25 MINUTES

1 cup all-purpose flour

Brimming ¼ cup sugar

1½ tablespoons cornstarch

2 teaspoons baking powder

2 teaspoons matcha powder

Rounded ¼ teaspoon fine
   sea salt

1 egg

¾ cup full-fat unsweetened
   coconut milk (shake or stir
   before using)

2 tablespoons virgin coconut
   oil, melted and cooled

1¼ teaspoons vanilla extract

Grassy with hints of vanilla and tea, pandan (aka screw pine) is one of the most alluring ingredients in tropical Vietnam. Its vibrant color and flavor imbue a lot of foods, including the popular waffles sold at many Little Saigon bakeries. Crisp on the outside and tender on the inside, the waffles are eaten like a cookie (no syrup is used).

The waffles' cheerful mint-green color is due to food coloring in the artificially flavored pandan extract, a convenient concentrate that's employed in Vietnam and abroad. Since the extract isn't widely available in America, I use culinary-grade matcha powder (it's affordable!). The Japanese green tea pairs well with vanilla and coconut to evoke the look and taste of pandan; only a little is used, otherwise the waffles scream *matcha* and you go into caffeine overdrive. Sure, these matcha "pandan" waffles aren't glowing green, but they're naturally flavored and colored, tasty, and fun to make whenever you're in the mood.

/

Preheat the waffle maker. Meanwhile, in a 4-cup measuring cup or a bowl, combine the flour, sugar, cornstarch, baking powder, matcha, and salt and whisk into a pale green mixture.

In a medium bowl, whisk together the egg, coconut milk, coconut oil, and vanilla. Pour the liquid ingredients into the dry ingredients and whisk vigorously until smooth, very thick, and sage green. Expect it to rise a bit. If you have time, let it rest for 5 minutes for a slightly smoother texture.

Pour the batter into the waffle maker, filling the wells until nearly overflowing (I use 1 cup for my Presto Belgian waffle maker). Cook for about 5 minutes, until the waffle is golden and verging on totally crisp. Remove the waffle with a fork or chopsticks and let cool on a wire rack for about 5 minutes to let it crisp up some more. Repeat with the remaining batter. When the waffles cool completely, they will lose a bit of their crispness. If the waffles aren't as crisp as you like them by the time you eat (or if you prefer crunchy waffles), heat them in a 350°F toaster oven or regular oven for 3 to 4 minutes.

Leave the waffles whole, or break them up to share, and serve.

BANANA-COCONUT bread-pudding cake

SERVES 6 TO 8

**TAKES 30 MINUTES,
PLUS 2½ HOURS TO BAKE
AND COOL**

1½ pounds overripe bananas

¼ cup dark rum

About ½ cup sugar

¼ teaspoon fine sea salt

One 13½-ounce can full-fat
  unsweetened coconut milk

2 tablespoons virgin
  coconut oil

1 teaspoon vanilla extract

1 egg

Generous 8 ounces white
  or wheat sandwich bread
  or supermarket French
  baguette, cut or torn into
  1-inch pieces, crust intact

Tons of bananas grow in Vietnam, which is why they appear in savories as well as sweets. This moist, fragrant, pudding-like cake is a great way to use overripe fruit or, in my case, a good reason to buy a big bunch at a good price and let some turn very dark and deliciously perfect for this treat.

There are many ways that Viet cooks make *bánh chuối*, but for this easy rendition, you need a slightly squishy, inexpensive bread. Supermarket sandwich bread or baguette is fine. Avoid fancy, rustic, or dense whole-grain breads because their sturdiness will dull the other flavors in this cake. Coconut goodness highlights the tropical nature of Viet cuisine. Instead of dark rum, my favorite spirit for this cake, you may try bourbon or brandy.

/

Peel and thinly slice the bananas, reserving 3 to 4 inches of one to decorate the top of the cake (choose the least blemished section!). In a medium bowl, combine the remaining bananas with the rum and 1½ tablespoons of the sugar and stir gently to mix. Set aside.

In a small saucepan, combine ⅓ cup sugar, the salt, coconut milk, coconut oil, and vanilla. Set over medium heat and cook, stirring or whisking, for 1 to 2 minutes to melt the oil and dissolve the sugar. In a large bowl, beat the egg and then whisk in the coconut milk mixture. Add the bread and stir to combine well. Set aside for 20 minutes to soften.

Meanwhile, preheat the oven to 375°F. Oil a 9-inch round cake pan with 2-inch sides, and line the bottom with parchment paper. (Or, use an 8-inch square pan.) Set aside.

When the bread is done soaking, use a potato masher to break up the chunks and create a thick, oatmeal-like mixture. Add the banana and its fragrant liquid and stir and fold to combine well. Pour the batter into the prepared pan, and shimmy the pan to level the top. Decorate with the reserved banana slices and sprinkle 1 teaspoon sugar all over the top.

/ CONTINUED

Bake for 1¼ to 1½ hours, until puffed up and richly browned. The top should feel dry to the touch and a toothpick or skewer inserted in the center should come out clean. Let cool on a wire rack for 1 hour (expect quick deflation), then run a blunt knife around the pan edge and unmold onto the rack. Remove the paper and reinvert onto a plate to showcase the attractive decorated side.

Enjoy the cake warm or let cool completely, to firm up, and eat at room temperature.

NOTES /

For big banana flavor and a more custardy texture, use slightly to very soft fruit. If the bananas are too firm, use a fork to poke four or five sets of holes in each one. Microwave in 30-second blasts, until barely soft. Cool to let the flesh further soften and sweeten before prepping.

Extra-rich coconut milk, such as Chaokoh brand (with 14 grams of fat per ⅓-cup serving), bakes up beautifully, promoting browning on the sides of the cake as well as the top. Inspect the nutrition label when choosing coconut milk for this recipe.

Cover and refrigerate leftovers for up to 3 days. Microwave slices in 20- to 30-second blasts to bring out the rum flavor. Or, bake in a 375°F toaster oven for 4 to 5 minutes and then broil for 1 to 2 minutes, until gently sizzling to re-crisp the top.

CASHEW SESAME *brittle*

MAKES ABOUT 8 OUNCES, TO SERVE 6

TAKES 45 MINUTES

Brimming ½ cup raw cashew halves and pieces

1 tablespoon raw sesame seeds (white, brown, or black)

¼ teaspoon fine sea salt

Scant 1 tablespoon virgin coconut oil

¼ teaspoon plus ⅛ teaspoon baking soda

½ cup sugar, preferably cane

⅓ cup light corn syrup

1 tablespoon water

Nut and seed brittles are a popular Vietnamese sweet, sold at bakeries and even airports. When I hanker for some, I make a small, fast batch to ensure its freshness. A candy thermometer doesn't work well with such a modest quantity. Instead, I carefully monitor the sugar syrup (no texting!) during the 10 minutes of cooking. My brittle has always turned out great, and I've become a better cook too.

Cashew halves and pieces lay flat and look handsome in brittle. The recipe calls for raw nuts and seeds, which yield nuanced flavor; if you use roasted ones, cut back on the final cooking a tad to avoid a burnt flavor.

/

To hold the hot brittle mixture, tear off a roughly 13-inch square piece of parchment paper and put on an inverted rimmed baking sheet, a wood cutting board, or the counter, if it is heat resistant. Have a rack ready for cooling.

In a medium bowl, combine the cashews, sesame seeds, salt, and coconut oil. Set near the stove with the baking soda.

In a heavy 1½- to 2-quart saucepan over medium heat, combine the sugar, corn syrup, and water. Bring to a boil, stirring constantly with a silicone spatula to dissolve the sugar. Continue boiling, stirring frequently, for 3 to 4 minutes, until the sugar mixture thickens a lot. When you dip the spatula in the pan and lift it out, some of the sugar will slide off, but a bubble-laden coating will remain. (This is the soft-crack stage, about 290°F on a candy thermometer.)

Dump the cashews, sesame seeds, salt, and coconut oil into the syrup and cook, stirring constantly, for about 2 minutes. The stiff mixture will soon loosen, turn foamy, and feel lighter under the weight of the spatula. When it's fragrant and the cashews have darkened a shade or two, remove the pan from the heat.

/ CONTINUED

Add the baking soda to the pan, stirring vigorously; the mixture will bubble, rise, and turn opaque. Immediately pour it onto the parchment paper and use the spatula to spread it out so it's roughly ¼ inch thick. Let sit for 5 minutes to set, then put the parchment on the rack to cool completely, about 30 minutes. Lift the brittle off the paper, check the underside, and, if needed, blot the bottom with paper towels to remove excess oil. Break the brittle into shards.

Eat soon or store in an airtight container at room temperature for up to 1 month.

NOTES /

Cane sugar works perfectly for this recipe. Beet sugar does not caramelize well.

If corn syrup isn't for you, substitute brown rice syrup (sold at many health food stores); it's cloudy and thick, so stir more often than recommended in the recipe, and feel free to occasionally slide the pan off the burner to check progress.

Try peanuts instead of cashews, and pumpkin seeds instead of sesame seeds.

When doubling the recipe, use a larger saucepan.

SILKY ORANGE-RUM *flan*

SERVES 4

**TAKES 1½ HOURS, PLUS AT
LEAST 5 HOURS TO CHILL**

1 large orange

Brimming 1 cup freshly
boiled water, plus
1 tablespoon water

⅓ cup plus 2 teaspoons
sugar, preferably cane

⅛ teaspoon unseasoned
rice vinegar or fresh lime
or lemon juice (optional,
but great for fuss-free
caramelization)

½ cup full-fat sweetened
condensed milk

1 egg, plus 2 egg yolks

2 tablespoons dark rum

Delicate and refreshing, this flan is a spin on one of my mom's recipes—part of the personal collection she brought from Vietnam when we fled in 1975. (The handwritten notebook inspired my food-writing career.) Mom's *bánh flan* recipe called for diluting a can of sweetened condensed milk with three cans of water, adding eggs, and cooking the custard mixture in a Chinese steamer. ("Fresh milk was hard to get in Vietnam," she explained, "and ovens were rare.") The result was light and silky. Although she didn't drink alcohol, she poured rum on the flan for a boozy finish.

For my updated version here, I make an orange infusion and combine it with dark rum to flavor the custard. Grated zest yields an interior with orange specks, so I infuse water with strips of orange zest. The resulting flan is fresh and elegant, a perfect way to end a Viet meal. For a gutsy alternative, make the Vietnamese coffee flan in the Notes.

/

Gently scrub the orange with a vegetable brush to remove any waxy coating (stop when you get a slight orangey whiff), quickly rinse, and pat dry. Use a vegetable peeler to remove strips of the zest, then cut into rough, confetti-like pieces; you want about 3 tablespoons. Transfer the zest to a heatproof bowl or measuring cup and add the brimming 1 cup water. Cover with a lid or plate and let steep for 20 to 30 minutes to create an orange-scented infusion.

Preheat the oven to 350°F. Select four 5- to 6-ounce ramekins, about 3½ inches in diameter and 1½ inches deep; ovenproof custard cups work too. Arrange the ramekins in a baking dish, then slide the baking dish into the oven. Warm molds are easier to coat evenly with hot caramel.

Meanwhile, in a small heavy-bottomed saucepan (one with a light interior is perfect for monitoring the caramelization), combine the 1 tablespoon water, sugar, and vinegar (if using). Set over medium heat and stir with a silicone spatula or metal spoon until the sugar nearly dissolves. Stop stirring and cook, undisturbed, and when the bubbling begins, cook for 4 to 5 minutes, until the sugar is light amber, the color of tea.

/ CONTINUED

Get ready for the slightly tricky part. Turn off the heat and keep the pan on the hot burner for 30 to 45 seconds, to allow the sugar to darken further to a dark amber (think a light-bodied red wine). Retrieve the baking dish from the oven (but keep the oven on) and set nearby.

When the caramel is ready, pour about 1 tablespoon into each ramekin. Using tongs, swirl the ramekins and fully coat the bottoms. (If the caramel sets rock hard before you get a chance to coat the bottom well, microwave the ramekin in 20-second blasts to melt the sugar and then swirl again.) Set the ramekins aside to cool; they can be slightly warm or room temperature when you add the custard, just not hot.

Bring a kettle of water to a boil, turning the heat to low to keep it hot, if needed.

In a measuring cup or small bowl, whisk together the sweetened condensed milk, egg, egg yolks, and rum. Set a fine-mesh strainer on top, then pour through the infused orange water to strain out the zest. Press on the zest to extract the oil, then discard. You should have 2 cups of custard; if you're shy, add tap water to make up the difference. Whisk the mixture until well combined but not frothy. Divide the mixture between the ramekins and return the ramekins to the baking dish. Pour enough hot water into the baking dish to come halfway up the sides of the ramekins.

Bake for 45 to 60 minutes, until a skewer or toothpick inserted in the middle of the custard comes out clean. Expect a little wobbliness in the center. The cooking time depends on the baking vessel material (ceramic, glass, or metal) and its thickness. Remove the baking dish from the oven, then transfer the ramekins to a wire rack to cool completely. Cover and refrigerate for at least 5 hours or up to 5 days to firm up and further develop flavor.

Before serving, let the flans sit at room temperature for at least 15 minutes or up to 1 hour to remove some, if not all, of the chill. There's bound to be caramel stuck to the bottom when you unmold; you can capture most of it by letting the ramekins sit in freshly boiled water until they feel warm, 3 to 6 minutes—use enough water to come halfway up the sides. Or, microwave the flan on high in 20- to 30-second blasts.

To unmold, run a knife around the sides of the ramekin to loosen the flan. Cover the top with an inverted, small rimmed dish. Holding both the dish and ramekin, flip them over to unmold the flan onto the dish and release the caramel sauce. If you don't hear a gentle plop, give the ramekin and dish several shakes to nudge the flan out. Repeat with the remaining flans. Serve with teaspoons to savor the flan and sauce.

NOTES /

Cane sugar tends to caramelize better than beet sugar.

Feel free to play with the flan flavor. For a lime-rum flan, use the zest from 3 or 4 limes. Or, steep 2 tablespoons packed coarsely grated peeled ginger in the water for a ginger-rum flan.

For a **Vietnamese coffee flan**, make a brimming 1 cup of inky, Vietnamese-style coffee (see page 224). Set aside until lukewarm or cold. Prep the caramel and coat the ramekins as directed. To make the custard, whisk together ½ cup sweetened condensed milk, 2 eggs, 1 egg yolk, and ¼ teaspoon vanilla extract. Add enough coffee to make 2 cups total, whisk to blend, then divide among the prepared ramekins. Bake for about 50 minutes. Cool, chill, and unmold as directed.

VIETNAMESE coffee

MAKES A BRIMMING ½ CUP

TAKES 5 MINUTES

3 tablespoons ground
medium-dark or dark roast
coffee, such as Café Du
Monde, or French, Italian,
or Spanish roast

About ⅔ cup hot water

Don't feel obligated to buy a traditional Vietnamese, metal coffee
filter to make authentic Viet coffee. The *phin* filter is charming but
slow, and not everyone in Vietnam uses it. The important thing to
focus on is making inky, slightly bitter, very strong-tasting coffee.
Use your favorite method. For a quick daily cup, I employ the
Aeropress, which some people compare to a French press but I see
it as a high-tech cousin of the *phin* filter.

This recipe makes a single serving to be combined with condensed
milk in one of the drink recipes that follow. For the milk, full-fat
Eagle Brand and Carnation are great substitutes for the Longevity
(Old Man) brand sold at Viet markets; or try coconut sweetened
condensed milk if you are vegan. No matter how it's made, Viet
coffee is a delicious heart thumper. Drink slowly.

/

Assemble the Aeropress with a metal or paper filter in place and set
over a coffee cup. Add the ground coffee, then shake the chamber
to distribute. Pour in 3 tablespoons of the hot water to moisten and
bloom the coffee. After the water passes through, about 30 seconds,
add the remaining ½ cup hot water. Stir five times, then wait for
the water to pass through until half of the original volume remains,
30 to 90 seconds. Slowly plunge to express the remaining coffee
before serving.

hot coffee with condensed milk

Add 1 tablespoon sweetened condensed milk to ½ cup hot coffee.
Stir well to create a caramel-colored drink. Taste and, if it's too
intense, splash in hot water to dilute.

iced coffee with condensed milk

Stir together ½ cup coffee with 2 tablespoons sweetened condensed
milk. Put 4 or 5 ice cubes in a tall glass. Pour the coffee over the ice
and stir with a long spoon or chopstick to chill and slightly dilute.

ABOUT THE AUTHOR

A bank examiner gone astray, **Andrea Nguyen** is living out her childhood dream of being an award-winning writer, editor, teacher, and consultant. Her impactful books—*Into the Vietnamese Kitchen*, *Asian Dumplings*, *Asian Tofu*, *The Banh Mi Handbook*, and *The Pho Cookbook*—have been recognized by the James Beard Foundation, International Association of Culinary Professionals, and National Public Radio for their excellence. She edited *Unforgettable*, a biography cookbook about culinary icon Paula Wolfert.

Andrea has contributed to many publications, including the *Washington Post*, *Wall Street Journal*, *Lucky Peach*, *Saveur*, and *Cooking Light*, where she is a monthly columnist. She earned bachelor's and master's degrees in finance and communication management from the University of Southern California, and studied at the Chinese University of Hong Kong.

Keep up with Andrea at Vietworldkitchen.com.

ACKNOWLEDGMENTS

Years of monitoring grocery-store inventories and interest in Asian cooking led to me writing this book. It's an expression of my love of Vietnamese food, cross-cultural cooking, and supermarket shopping. My parents, Hoang and Tuyet Nguyen, taught me how to shop wisely and cook thoughtfully. Along with my husband, Rory, they indulged and supported my long-term efforts to move Viet foodways from the margins into the mainstream.

This book idea was a no-brainer to my family, just as it was to my enthusiastic group of volunteer recipe testers, many of whom have worked with me on most of my cookbooks. A big thanks to these folks for following my recipes, trying them out on others, and providing honest feedback:

Linh Bui	Colin Hart	Daniel Nguyen
Diane Carlson	Cary Hart	Jenny Sager
Alex Ciepley	Kate Leahy	Karen Shinto
Jay Dietrich	Laura McCarthy	Terri Tanaka
Alyce Gershenson	Hugh McElroy	Catherine Thome
Candy Grover	Cate McGuire	Maki Tsuzuki
Doug Grover	Rosemary Metzger	Tina Ujlaki
Paulina Haduong	Josie Nevitt	Dave Weinstein

Ditto to the community at Vietworldkitchen.com and on social media. Your comments, likes, and loves added extra wind to my sails!

At Ten Speed Press, Aaron Wehner, editor Kelly Snowden, designer Betsy Stromberg, production designer Mari Gill, production manager Jane Chinn, and publicity pros Windy Dorresteyn, David Hawk, and Allison Renzulli championed this project from beginning to end. To make a visually compelling book, they brought together a dream team comprising photographer Aubrie Pick, assisted by Bessma Khalaf; food stylist Karen Shinto, assisted by Kate Leahy; and prop stylist Claire Mack.

Vietnamese food has come a long way since my family came to America in 1975. Thanks to all who've joined me on this journey.

INDEX

Published in the United States by Ten Speed Press, an imprint of the
Crown Publishing Group, a division of Penguin Random House LLC, New York.
www.crownpublishing.com
www.tenspeed.com

Ten Speed Press and the Ten Speed Press colophon are registered
trademarks of Penguin Random House LLC.

Library of Congress Cataloging-in-Publication Data
    Names: Nguyen, Andrea Quynhgiao, author.
    Title: Vietnamese food any day : simple recipes for true, fresh flavors /
        Andrea Quynhgiao Nguyen ; photography by Aubrie Pick.
    Description: California : Ten Speed Press, 2019. | Includes index.
    Identifiers: LCCN 2018017922 |
    Subjects: LCSH: Cooking, Vietnamese. | LCGFT: Cookbooks.
    Classification: LCC TX724.5.V5 N477 2019 | DDC 641.59597—dc23
    LC record available at https://lccn.loc.gov/2018017922

Hardcover ISBN: 978-0-399-58035-2
eBook ISBN: 978-0-399-58036-9

Printed in China

Design by Betsy Stromberg
Food styling by Karen Shinto
Prop styling by Claire Mack

10 9 8 7 6 5 4 3 2 1

First Edition